WHAT DRIVES WINNING

By Brett Ledbetter

Printed in the United States of America.

Books may be purchased in quantity and/or special sales by contacting Green Dot Publishing at info@greendotpub.com or visiting www.GreenDotPub.com.

Library of Congress Control Number: 2015905963

ISBN: 978-0-9962264-0-0

Cover and interior design by Lisa Kuntz

Editing by Cherry Pickman

FIRST EDITION

10 9 8 7 6 5

TABLE OF CONTENTS

Author's Note:
The names and identifying details concerning some individuals, as well as some elements of these individuals' stories, have been changed to protect their privacy.

Who you become as a result of the chase
is the most important thing.

– Dr. Jim Loehr

---

*Jim: thank you for being a strong,
positive force in my life. Our many conversations
have helped me understand the power of
repurposing sport to build character.*

A Special Thank-You:

To all of the athletes and coaches that I've
worked with and learned from.

WHAT DRIVES WINNING

Here's my favorite question to ask players in our basketball academy:

What are the first two questions that you get asked after a game by someone who wasn't at the game?

The reason I like asking that question is because everybody has the same two answers:

1. Did you win?
2. How many points did you score?

Think about your sport. What are the questions you get asked? I come across a lot of athletes. Golfers will say, "What'd you shoot?" Pitchers are asked, "How many strikeouts?" Wide receivers are asked, "How many touches did you get?"

What does this show? It shows what society values. We are conditioned, at an early age, that results are what matter most.

That's why, when I was a senior in high school, I would write down on a piece of paper the goals that I wanted to accomplish every game. The paper would look something like this:

35 Points / 5 Rebounds / 5 Assists

At halftime, I'd pull out the piece of paper to see exactly what I needed to focus on for the second half. There are a bunch of different things wrong with the goals that I set (see: "Unselfish").

The point of that story is to show you how goal-oriented I was at an early age. That is, until I met a guy by the name of Don Meyer. At the time, Don was the all-time winningest coach in the history of men's college basketball. I asked him his thoughts on goals and here's what he told me:

I'm not real big on goals. We just wanted to make sure that we had the best practice we could every day.

Have you ever had a coach tell you to not set goals? That confused the heck out of me. But there were other high-level coaches that were saying the same thing.

Brad Stevens, an NBA coach, told me, "I've gone away from talking about goals with my team."

Why would a coach actually go away from talking about goals with their team?

Goals

Here's a definition of the word goal:

Goal: the result to which effort is aimed.

When you focus on goals, what do you focus on? Results. If you think about it, results are oftentimes outside of our control. For example, let's say you have a goal of scoring 35 points per game.

What are some things that could get in the way of you scoring 35 points that are out of your control?

- The opposing coach could decide to double-team you.
- Your teammate could get hot and become the best option.
- Refs are human. You could get in foul trouble early.

Do you see how none of these are fully in your control? So, the championship coaches that I'm around focus their energy on the second portion of the definition:

The result to which **effort is aimed.**

The Process

When you focus on the **effort aimed** at the result, you focus your energy on the things that you can control. We call the second portion of the definition "The Process." Your process is what drives your result.

We have a lot of high-level coaches that come in and observe our process. They watch the way that we teach footwork in our academy. We've developed a scientific approach that breaks down the movements of the game into manageable steps in a way that almost anybody can learn.

When these coaches come into watch, they're amazed at how our players move. They all say the same thing, *"I can't believe that you're getting players to move like that."* We see that. But we also see that it doesn't transition into the game for everyone.

So we started to ask why.

We've found that there are many different reasons, but here's one reason: a player struggles with confidence.

Why would we think that a player would want to go out in front of a 1,000—maybe even 5,000—people and perform at the risk of looking bad in front of all of those people? No player wants to do that. And it's our job as coaches to help players trust themselves in those pressurized situations.

It's evident that there's something else that's driving the process. That's exactly what I talked to Mike "Coach K" Krzyzewski about. Coach K is the Duke men's basketball coach, and he's passed Don Meyer as college basketball's winningest coach.

I asked Coach K, "What drives the process?" He told me, "Character drives everything. When you have good character it drives it up. And when you have bad character, it drives it down. Character is the foundation upon which you win."

We believe that character is the foundation upon which you develop. We're going to show you how.

Separate the Person From the Player

A championship coach once told me, "I think coaches get distracted by the process and that prevents them from seeing what's really important."

Who drives the process? Human beings.

For example, let's say a coach develops an amazing skill-development plan for a player. The coach and the player both agree that this process is exactly what the player needs in order to achieve a specific goal.

What happens if the player doesn't have the discipline to execute the plan? Is the problem with the plan? Where does the breakdown occur?

The breakdown usually occurs with the person that is driving this process. Any time I work with an athlete, the first thing I do is separate the person from the player.

I explain: "The process that we've developed to help you get better is going to help you improve as a player. But your character is what's going to drive that process, and we are going to spend a lot of time developing who you are as a person."

For that to happen, the first thing we have to do is define what the word character means to us. Everybody has a different definition, so we want to make sure that we (myself and the player I'm working with) share the same meaning of the word. We've come up with a working definition that's simple and straightforward.

Character: who you are **as a person.**

Two Types

We believe that character comes in two types:

Performance Skills: character skills that govern your relationship with yourself.

These are the skills that will get you up at 5:30 a.m. to go work out in a gym by yourself just to get better.

Moral Skills: character skills that govern your relationship with others.

These are the skills that make you a great teammate and a great friend.

Think of it this way: **Performance skills get you to the top. Moral skills keep you there.**

The reason we say character "skills" not character "traits" is because of a conversation that I had with Carol Dweck who authored a great book called *Mindset*. She said, "Traits sound fixed."

We believe that all of these skills can be developed. That's why we call them skills. Therefore we believe that character can be developed.

The Character Study

A lot of the players at our Academy want to be college basketball players. So here's what we did. We boiled a little study down to these 15 championship basketball coaches:

Bill Self *University of Kansas*	**Jay Wright** *Villanova University*	**Tom Izzo** *Michigan State University*
Mike Krzyzewski *Duke University*	**Roy Williams** *North Carolina*	**Billy Donovan** *University of Florida**
Don Meyer *Northern State University*	**Brad Stevens** *Butler University**	**Mark Few** *Gonzaga University*
Jim Boeheim *Syracuse University*	**Muffet McGraw** *University of Notre Dame*	**Sherri Coale** *University of Oklahoma*
Geno Auriemma *University of Connecticut*	**John Beilein** *University of Michigan*	**Thad Matta** *Ohio State*

*Has since moved on to the NBA.

I interviewed each of them (some numerous times), and based on these interviews we determined the character skills that they most value in their players. We populated a list of the top 10 performance and the top 10 moral skills that they talked about. Here's the list:

CHARACTER SKILLS

PERFORMANCE	MORAL
Hardworking	Unselfish
Competitive	Honest
Positive	Respectful
Focused	Appreciative
Accountable	Humble
Resilient	Loyal
Confident	Trustworthy
Energetic	Encouraging
Disciplined	Socially Aware
Motivated	Caring

When you look at this list, think about teams you've been on. Think about teams you lead. What if every member of your team possessed these skills? How much better would you be?

As we were compiling the data, I remember thinking to myself, "We are teaching the wrong things. If everybody had these skills, they'd be great no matter what." It was this character study that changed the way that I work with our athletes. We then began to take this across other sports and realized that the best coaches, regardless of the sport, were coaching a different game.

What Drives Winning

Am I saying that you shouldn't set goals? No. (We'll cover that shortly.) Here's what I'm saying:

The championship coaches that I've been around focus less on the results and more on the process, but they realize that

character is what drives the process, which drives the result.

To illustrate it simply:

Character > Process > Result

Once we uncovered this C > P > R model, the journey towards building the person began.

Important: That does not mean that these coaches don't care about results. They do. Results matter. They just invest their energy into what drives the results.

PART I

A look into the C > P > R model

1

Person > Player

Person > Player

Meet Blakely. She's a remarkable young lady that I've been working with. She plays soccer. I don't know much about soccer. Here's what I do know: we related on a deeper level. We shared the same story. And as I started to share our story, I realized that there were a lot of people who could relate.

Quick background: Blakely started playing soccer at thirteen years old (that's really late to start a sport). Six years later, here's her resumé:

> Division I Scholarship
> National Freshman of the Year
> Starter: U20 National Team

The day before we met for the first time, I had her write down what she was struggling with the most. Here's the note that she wrote me (see if you can relate):

My biggest struggle is dealing with expectations. I set my standards so high personally that it's not okay to fail, but it should be. I haven't been able to accept that yet. I've had a lot of success through my soccer, especially this past year. So how do I match or exceed that so I don't let people down?

So many people from family, friends, coaches, teammates, and media all expect something from me. They want success. And when I'm not succeeding they don't want any part of it. If I don't maintain my play, my characteristics, my purity, if I make a mistake everyone is watching. Judging.

It feels like they're waiting for me to fail so they can say, "I told you so..." or "She's not the 'Golden girl' that everyone thought she was." For me, it's everything. I feel watched, pressured, and judged for every little thing I do or say.

I can't say that I'm not grateful for that because this is what brought me success. It's what made me, I guess, "popular" in the soccer world. But with that comes so much pressure. I'm scared to fail. I can't fail. I can't fail for my family. I can't fail for my coaches (past or present). I can't fail for my teammates. I can't fail for all of the people who told me that I couldn't do it. I can't fail for myself.

As you can see, she's dealing with a lot of pressure. So the following day I asked her three questions:

Me: Do you feel like your identity is tied to the result of your performance on the field?

Blakely: Absolutely.

Me: Do you see how results are outside of your control?

Blakely: Yes.

Me: Do you see how you're allowing something that's outside of your control to affect the way you feel about yourself as a person?

Blakely: Yes.

In the next section, we'll talk about how it gets to this point. Before we go there, I asked her three more questions to try and expand her perspective. (We asked our basketball academy these same three questions. Try answering them for yourself.)

Me: Who was the leading goal scorer in the NCAA three years ago?

Blakely: I don't know.

Me: That's interesting. Who was your favorite teacher growing up?

Blakely: My eighth-grade science teacher.

Me: Why?

Blakely: She was really personable and she got to know us.

What does Blakely's answer tell us about her eighth-grade science teacher? She was great at connecting and building relationships. And that's exactly what Blakely remembers about her. I can relate. My fourth-grade teacher was my favorite. I was ten years old when I was in her class. I'm thirty years old now and I still have lunch with her every couple months. It's amazing the impact a good teacher can have.

Why do people pick the teachers that they do? Here are the most common answers we got from our Academy:

1. They made learning fun.
2. They challenged me.
3. They were supportive.
4. They were helpful.
5. They got to know me.

What do you think the purpose of the three questions that I asked Blakely were:

1. Leading goal scorer?
2. Favorite teacher?
3. Why?

What do these questions show?

What do people forget? People forget stats.

What do people remember? They remember who you were as a person.

So I asked Blakely to write down how she wants to be remembered. Here's exactly what she said:

I want to be remembered as the girl whose character never swayed and remained true in every aspect. When little girls come to watch me play, I want them to be able to say, "I want to be the PERSON she is... not just the soccer player." Like you told me earlier, people will forget stats. They will forget how many goals I scored. But they will always remember the person that I was and my true character.

It's important to note that this is exactly what Blakely wrote. There were no edits made (for this book) and I wasn't present when she was writing it. Which word jumps off the page? Person, right? She put that word in all-caps. Why would she do that?

She's making it very clear what's most important to her. When I saw this, I knew we had something special and we could go to work. Here's what we created—a new grading system:

Person > Player

The person is more important than the player. And, ultimately, the person drives the player (more on that to come).

We then created a supporting sentence. Anytime younger girls come to watch her play, here's the thought that we want them to leave with: I want to be the PERSON she is, not just the soccer player.

We made cards that look like this: (See next page.)

Person $\rangle$ Player

*I want to be the PERSON she is...
not just the soccer player.*

She's putting them everywhere. Her phone. Her mirror. Her Gatorade bottle. Why? She needs a constant reminder, because this is exactly the opposite of how she has been conditioned. Here's why this matters:

In soccer, missing a penalty kick is similar to missing a clutch free-throw in basketball. So, let's say that Blakely misses a penalty kick. If her identity is tied to how she performs as a player, then how is she feeling in that moment? Terrible, right? Is she in a good state of mind to move forward to the next play? No.

But, what if we switch the grading system? What if we graded her as a person? What if we graded how she handled the missed penalty kick? If we can shift her identity back to herself as a person, we can then repurpose that moment and make it something bigger. That missed penalty kick now becomes an opportunity to show the younger girls (and her teammates) how to handle failure.

Do you see that? And if she handles failure better, do you see how that will actually get her to the next play faster? So focusing on who she wants to be as a person actually helps her become a better player in the process.

And on the flipside, let's say she scores a goal to win the game. What can she now show those younger girls (and her teammates)? She can show them how to handle success with humility. Do you see that?

Now our job is to repurpose everything that happens to her in soccer *as a player* as an opportunity to grow *as a person*. Because who you become as a result of chasing your goals is the most important thing, and we're trying to move her closer to the person she ultimately wants to become. And, as you'll soon see, it's a tremendous challenge.

What's Holding You Back?

Here's a question that I love asking players: Are the forces of sport moving you closer or further away from the person that you want to become?

Unfortunately for a lot of us, the pressure that comes with sports brings out the worst in us. We've all been in situations through our sport where we've gone negative or lost our confidence. Or even become selfish to achieve our goals. I think it's critical for us to use the powerful forces of sport to move us closer to the person that we want to become.

In order to do that, we have to know what's getting in the way. I've talked with a lot of athletes—from tiny 5th graders just beginning their sport, to the best high school players in the country, to the best athletes at major Division I universities, to professional athletes.

You know what they all have in common? They are human beings. They deal with similar issues that prevent them from being at their best—they're just on different levels.

Through my work, I've developed a list of the most common barriers we see that get in the way of them being their best. Anytime I work with athletes, I give them this checklist (pictured on the next page) and ask them to check off the things that they struggle with. Most likely, there will be a lot of checkmarks. That's OK.

After they fill the list out, I have them go back through and rank in order the top five things that they struggle with most (1 being what they struggle with the most). This gives us a road map, and sets us up for the next activity.

Challenge: What do you struggle with that's preventing you from being all that you can be?

WHAT'S HOLDING YOU BACK?

Name: _____

- Comparing yourself to others
- Consumed by results
- Getting over mistakes
- Expectations from others (parents, coaches, peers)
- Confronting people
- Identity outside of sport (Who am I?...without my sport)
- Fear of failure
- Lack of motivation
- I listen to the wrong voice in my head (I'm negative)
- Dealing with pressure
- Playing free
- The inability to ever please myself (Never happy with my accomplishments)
- Understanding my purpose for playing
- Not having a relationship with myself
- Dealing with outside criticism
- Self-doubt (Lack of confidence)
- Care too much about recognition and status (Upholding reputation)
- Understanding team success is more important than my individual success
- Emotional control (Frustration, anger, etc.)
- Self-worth tied to performance
- Interpersonal relationships (Coaches / Teammates / Peers)

- Time management (Prioritization)
- Expectations I have for myself
- Care too much about what others think about me
- Controlling parents
- Keeping love for the game
- Accepting constructive criticism from teammates / coaches
- Giving constructive criticism to teammates
- Urge to be perfect
- Being able to adapt in a new environment
- Loneliness
- Fear of success
- Judgement (from self and others)
- Judgmental towards other people
- Work ethic
- Seeking validation from others
- Struggle with trusting others
- Not being accepted
- Leaving my comfort zone
- Losing perspective of all the great opportunities sport brings me
- Making excuses (Not going "all-in")
- Accepting my role
- Discipline to stick to a plan
- Keeping my personal problems away from the court/field/gym/pool, etc.

Other _____

Goal Achievement

I asked Blakely to write down the goals that she has for her upcoming sophomore year. Here's what she wrote down:

My goals:
Win Conference Championship
Win National Championship
Beat Scoring Record

We had a conversation about her goals. Here's how it went:

Me: Why is accomplishing those goals important?

Blakely: To feel successful.

Me: Why is that important?

Blakely: It's what everyone works for.

Me: Why is that important?

Blakely: It gives you a sense of achievement.

Me: Why is that important?

Blakely: Reaching success makes you happy.

That's exactly where we needed to go. We've been conditioned to think this. When I asked everybody in our Academy, "How many of you believe that when you hit your goals, that brings happiness?" Everybody raised their hands.

Happiest Girl Alive

Blakely started playing soccer at thirteen years old. Again, that's really late to start a sport. So I asked her a question: "What if I met you when you were thirteen years old and I told you that you would accomplish these things by age nineteen:"

> Division 1 Scholarship
> National Freshman of the Year
> Starter: U20 National Team

"How would that make you feel?"

Blakely responded, "I'd be the happiest girl alive."

Here's what's interesting: that's the exact situation that she's in.

So I asked her, "Are you the happiest girl alive?"

She said, "No."

Isn't that interesting? She has everything that she thought she would want, yet she still feels empty and unfulfilled.

Happiness versus Fulfillment

When you accomplish your goals, you feel a spike in excitement. That feeling is addictive. So addictive, in fact, that we start to chase it. That feeling is happiness. Here's how we define happiness to the players in our Academy:

Happiness: short-term pleasure.

The excitement of happiness doesn't last long-term. And, for most people, it's tied to the outcome.

For example:

I play well = I'm happy.
I don't play well = I'm not happy.

Which makes sense; it's hard to be happy when you don't play well. But then you're allowing the way you feel to be determined by a result that isn't fully within your control.

How do we enjoy the journey? What are we looking for? We are looking for fulfillment. Here's our definition:

Fulfillment: satisfaction from developing one's ability or character.

In other words, when we start to prioritize the growth of who we are becoming as a person (over the result) that's where we find fulfillment. That's how we overcome the feeling of being empty.

I Feel Empty

Did you know that a lot of the championship coaches that I've talked to experience depression after winning a championship? I ask our players, "Why do you think that is?"

Here's a great story (from a player's perspective) to illustrate why that is:

A player just won a state championship as a junior in high school. That night, he celebrated with his team—everyone was happy. The next day, they drove back to their high school. As this player got off of the bus, he was greeted by a group of people.

The group asked the player, "Are you going to repeat next year?"

And just like that, the expectation had been set. All of a sudden, he felt the weight of everybody's expectations.

As he reflected he thought, *I spent the last year of my life chasing this championship and the happiness that I felt from that championship lasted less than a day. It felt like everything was back to normal.*

A Championship Rose

Anson Dorrance gives his soccer players at the University of North Carolina roses after they win a national championship. He's won over twenty of them as a head coach.

I asked him why he did that.

He told me, "I'm actually not really big on championship rings or trophies. I prefer flowers. The reason I give them a rose is because it's ephemeral—the rose dies and it dies relatively quickly."

To Anson, the rose is a symbol of the championship feeling that fades away quickly. It helps his players realize that the pleasure that comes with the accomplishment is not a part of who they are. It's just a cool thing that they did.

The best analogy that I try to give people is to have them imagine a family vacation. Think about a cool destination. You're looking forward to it and you're thinking, "Man, I can't wait. This is going to be awesome."

Then you get there, and you realize something. You realize that you are exactly the same person, with the same problems, just in a different location.

A 3rd Grader's Dream

We've been conditioned to chase goals. And I'm not saying that's a bad thing. Here's an example: As a 3rd Grader, NBA player Gordon Hayward wrote a goal checklist with the help of his dad. Together they wrote down a road map of goals. The checklist read:

- ☐ NBA
- ☐ Division 1 College
- ☐ Varsity Basketball
- ☐ 8th Grade Team
- ☐ 7th Grade Team
- ☐ 6th Grade Team
- ☐ 5th Grade Team
- ☐ 4th Grade Team
- ☐ 3rd Grade Team

They kept the list. The night Gordon was drafted to the NBA, he and his dad checked off *NBA*.

After they accomplished the goal of making the NBA, what did they do? They made a new one: *Win a World Championship.*

This is a great example—that even when we reach our dreams, the chase never stops.

Don Meyer versus Mike Krzyzewski

To refresh: when I met Don Meyer he was number one on the all-time wins list in men's college basketball. Do you remember what he said? He said, "I'm not real big on goals. We just wanted to have the best practice we could every day."

He also added, "There's no need to put needless pressure on yourself by setting goals like that."

For me, I put a ton of pressure on myself, so I really liked that idea and thought, "You know what? I'm not real big on goals either." I embraced the idea.

Then something happened. I talked with Mike Krzyzewski. Mike just passed Don Meyer on the wins list—he's now number one.

I said to him, "You know, a lot of coaches have gone away from talking about goals with their teams. Is that true for you?"

He said, "No. I'm still very much goal-oriented."

Right when I got to a point where I was like, "OK, I don't think I'm big on goals," Mike confused the heck out of me. This kept me up for weeks.

Here's what I did: I talked to Carol Dweck. Carol's a Stanford psychologist who wrote a book called *Mindset*.

I asked, "How could two of the most successful coaches have such a different stance on goals?"

She answered, "In sports, goals are clearly defined. In life, it's much more ambiguous. You have to have something to point your energy at."

What does that mean? I asked our Academy to break down what Carol said.

1st line: In sports goals are clearly defined.

What does society use to determine whether or not we are successful? The scoreboard. In relationships, do you keep score? Obviously you don't. (If you do, you should probably see a couples' therapist.)

2nd Line: In life, it's much more ambiguous.

Ambiguous means not clearly defined. In other words, there are so many different paths that you can take in life.

3rd Line: You have to have something to point your energy at.

Goals can narrow your focus and help you point your energy toward one path.

3 Phases of Goals

I've had an interesting relationship with goals for the last fifteen years of my life. I've gone through three phases. See if you can relate to this:

1st Phase: I Loved Goals

This was when I was younger. In my eyes, on the other side of that goal was success. When you reach your goals, how does it make you feel? You feel the excitement. As we talked about, that feeling doesn't last long. So what do you do? You set another goal. You start learning to chase that feeling.

But here's what starts to happen. When you become better at your sport things change. Let's say you score 30 points in a basketball game. What do your peers now expect from you every game? They expect 30 points. That's where I entered the 2nd phase.

2nd **Phase: I Hated Goals**

My goals started to become determined by other people's expectations. Other people were setting my goals for me indirectly. I hated that. It caused a high level of anxiety because I knew that I wasn't fully in control of the result. In this phase, I was worried about things outside of my control and whether or not I could please everybody around me.

As we saw in an earlier example:

What is outside of my control that would affect me scoring 30 points?

> - Aspects of my coach's strategy that don't involve me scoring.
> - The defensive strategy of the other team could be to double or triple-team me.
> - Getting in foul trouble.

3rd **Phase: I Understood Goals**

I started to understand goals. It was never the goals that I had the issue with. It was the relationship that I had with the pressure that comes with goals. How did I look at pressure?

I looked at it as a threat. If I don't hit the goal, what am I? I'm a failure. My identity and self-worth was attached to whether or not I hit my goals.

Once I realized that I needed to change my relationship with pressure, things changed for me.

I learned how to convert the pressure that comes with goals (from a threat) into an opportunity. How did I do that? I began to use the energy pressure creates as an opportunity to grow into a better player and, most importantly, a stronger person.

Is Pressure Your Enemy?

Do you struggle with pressure? Do you view it as a threat and does it bring out the worst in you? How can we change that? When we learn to appreciate pressure, we turn it into a partner rather than an enemy. Here's how I start that conversation with players. We ask them:

When are you more likely to study for a test?

- The night before the test?
- A week out from the test?

When I ask players this question, what do you think they say? Nearly every one of them says the night before the test. The tight deadline creates pressure, which leads to a sense of urgency.

I then ask them, "What if there wasn't a test? Would you study?"

They start laughing. Why? Because they know they wouldn't.

What does this show?

Pressure creates an urgency that can help us with our development.

Thank You, Pressure

Here's one way you can learn how to appreciate pressure—write a thank-you note to it.

Here's an example of one player's note:

Dear Pressure:

Thank you for making me better. You know how to expose and challenge me more than anybody in my life. I know that we haven't always had the best relationship, but now that I reflect, I realize that it's my fault. I wouldn't have been able to get to the level that I'm at…without your help.

I've learned that, like any friend, I need short breaks from you. When I have separation from you, I realize how much I miss you and how much you do for me. Then I'm ready to get back together and accept your challenge. Thank you for teaching me about myself—you've provided me with so many lessons that have made me a stronger person.

Thank you for taking me to a level that I could have never gotten to on my own!

Do you see how this player converted pressure into a friend? Could you do the same? The best way to view pressure as an opportunity is to appreciate all that it does for your growth.

Challenge: Reflect and write a thank-you note to pressure to see how it's helped you. Take your time when you do. It might unlock a new perspective.

Fear of Failure

A player called me and asked me for some advice. He told me that he just got done playing his first game of the season and he didn't play up to his own standards. He was struggling mentally.

I asked, "How can I help?"

The player said, "I really want to be a McDonalds All-American and I feel so much pressure."

I asked, "Are you afraid of failure?"

He quickly responded, "Yes."

Here's how we define failure: not reaching your goal.

Why do people fear failure? People fear failure when they attach their self-worth to achievement. When this happens, *what they do becomes who they are.*

Here's what that sounds like:

"I am a failure because I didn't reach my goal of becoming a McDonalds All-American."

Instead of:

"I failed reaching my goal of becoming a McDonalds All-American."

In the second statement, you've distanced yourself as a person from the achievement (or failure) as a player.

This player attached his self-worth to the goal. When this happens, do you see how this player unravels and questions everything about his life after one bad game? We needed to undress the truth.

Undressing the Truth

Me: Why is it important for you to be a McDonalds All-American?

Player: I've wanted it since I was a freshman.

Me: Why?

Player: If you get it—it means you're good.

Me: So it validates you?

Player: Yes.

Me: So you're chasing validation?

Player: Wait, no. (Pause) I don't know what I'm chasing.

It's Never Enough

Here's what's interesting: this player has won three straight state championships. Yet, in his mind, he needed more validation. Why?

I asked this player, "What if I met you when you were ten years old and I told you that you would lead your team to three straight state championships. What would you tell me?"

Player: Wow.

Me: Do you think that would have made you feel like you were successful?

Player: Yes.

Here's the situation: this player is likely to go down as the state's all-time winningest player and he is still chasing a feeling of validation.

Why does this happen? I tried to help this player understand:

Me: Can I ask you something? Have you ever studied hard for a test and got an A?

Player: Yes.

Me: How long did that feeling of accomplishment last?

Player: A few minutes.

Me: Why did it go away?

Player: I started to think about the next thing.

Do you see how quickly that feeling of accomplishment fades away?

This player wants to be a McDonalds All-American (and that's great to strive for), but do you think that will satisfy him? What will happen next? He'll want something else. Just like Gordon Hayward. When he checked the box: *Play in the NBA*, what'd he do next? He set another goal to chase.

The "Why" Behind the Goal

Player: Are you saying that I shouldn't set the goal of becoming a McDonalds All-American?

Me: No. I think it's good to have something to chase. It accelerates your growth.

Player: So goals are good? Is that what you are saying?

Me: I'm saying that the **"why" behind the goal** is more important than the goal itself.

Player: Can you give me an example?

In this case the player's goal is to become a McDonalds All-American. Why? He wants it for status and validation.

Here's a better "why": to narrow my focus and challenge myself to develop as a player and as a person so I can use my experience to help others.

Do you see how that could lead to fulfillment?

We've changed the game. The goal creates the chase. Why is that important? It's important for growth.

When we attach our "why" to something external like status, recognition, or validation it's not lasting and we start to chase the next thing.

When we attach our "why" to growth, we feel fulfilled regardless of the result. Why? Growth is long-term.

My Conclusion on Goals

When you set an external goal it creates something. What does it create? It creates a chase. When you have something to chase it:

- Creates pressure (make sure you view it as your friend).
- Narrows your focus.
- Accelerates your growth.

The "why" behind your chase is the most important thing. If you chase things externally to help you grow internally, then it becomes a productive challenge. I believe that **who we become as a result of the chase is the most important thing.**

The real goal: personal growth to help others.

2

Getting the Order Right

Write a Letter to Your Sport

What does the word **discover** mean? It means *to find something unexpected in the course of a search.* One of the most important things that I do is help people discover things about themselves that they didn't know. We call it self-discovery. And we start by exploring the relationship that they have with their sport.

Dr. Jim Loehr, author of *The Only Way To Win,* has had such a strong impact on me. He's helped me understand character on a deeper level. One day we were talking and he told me an awesome exercise to do with players. He said, "Have your players write a letter to their sport as if it's a person. Have them describe the impact that it's had on their life—good or bad."

That evening, I called Napheesa, a very high-level athlete, and asked her to do the exercise. Here's her letter to basketball:

Dear Basketball:

Even though we've had our ups and downs, I'm still so thankful I found you. You have given me some of the best moments of my life. Although I've had to sacrifice a lot for you like parties, sleepovers, and summer in general, you have given me so much more in return.

You're the reason I'll be able to go to the college of my choice, the reason that I've been able to travel to so many amazing places, and most importantly, you're the reason that I've made so many lifelong friends.

Thank you basketball,
Napheesa

I loved her letter, especially the first line: *we've had our ups and downs.* She recognized that it hasn't all been good. She also wrote, *I've had to sacrifice a lot for you like…summer in general.* There was a period where she was out of town for sixteen weekends in the summer—for someone who enjoys socializing, that's quite a commitment.

I decided to write a letter to basketball as well.

Dear Basketball,

As a player, you gave me a purpose—a reason to reject social norms and carve my own path. I will always cherish the times we spent alone on Friday/Saturday nights when I didn't want to go to parties. You gave me a place to go when I was frustrated. You taught me about success. You taught me about failure. You motivated me to be better and through you I learned so much through the joy and pain that you caused me.

Now, you are the vehicle that allows me to help other people. And I've met so many wonderful people through you. You've put me in a position to pass on all of the lessons that I've learned through you to people so they can better understand their relationship with you. I'm very thankful for all of the success and adversity that I experienced from you—it has made me the person that I am today.

Love,
Brett

The more athletes I come across, the more I enjoy doing this exercise. It helps me gauge whether or not their relationship is healthy. I had this player write a letter to his sport and incorporate the top 5 things that are holding him back. I asked him to explain to his sport (as if it were a person) how it is moving him further away from the person he wants to be. Take a look at this letter he wrote to golf:

Dear Golf,

I feel very blessed that I was introduced to you. You always give me something to strive for and an opportunity to improve myself. For that, I thank you. But, sometimes I can get very mad at you. I'm trying to understand that the challenges you bring me are there to make me stronger—sometimes I lose perspective of that. I think my father gets in the way of me seeing things clearly. It's like he's a third wheel.

For a long time I thought my identity was in you. I relied on you too much to feel good about myself. Lately I have been trying to learn how to separate my identity from you. Relying on you to feel good about myself can be damaging for me because you are simply too unreliable.

I think I need to learn who I am without you. I still want you to be a huge part of my life, but I am going to work hard at learning more about myself without you. But I want you to know that I am very thankful for our relationship. Some of the greatest moments of my life are times I spent with you.

There's a big difference between these two statements:

"I'm a _____." (Fill in the blank: golfer, basketball player, football player, etc.)

"I play _____." (Fill in sport: golf, basketball, football, etc.)

When you write a letter to your sport, you separate yourself from the sport. That's why I really like having players write letters to their sport; they are forced to distance themselves from the sport by viewing it as another person. By doing so, it allows me to see the impact that their sport is having.

After reading this player's letter, I knew exactly where we needed to go.

Getting the Order Right

My grandma has only been mad at me once in my life. It was because of a shirt that I wore. The shirt said *Basketball is life. The rest is just details.*

She looked at the shirt and said, "That's a bad shirt."

I couldn't understand why she would say that. I liked the shirt. After she told me her opinion, I remember that I had told her, "I'd rather die than live and not be able to play basketball."

She looked at me and said, "Brett, that's a bad statement." She thought that I didn't get it.

What did I think? I thought she didn't get it.

In my mind at the time, basketball was my life. And as crazy as this might sound to some, it made sense to me, to think that there was really no reason to live if I couldn't do what I loved. And nobody could convince me otherwise.

Now I want to introduce you to another perspective. That perspective is from Kyrie Irving. Kyrie is an NBA All-Star. He told me:

Kyrie Irving, NBA Player

Never think that basketball is the world. My dad always told me that basketball is a privilege, it's not a right—it can be taken away from you just like that. That's what I understood: I had to take care of my priorities in life first. Then, basketball comes natural. That's what I do. But life, I live that.

I love when Kyrie says, "Basketball is what I do." He doesn't say, "Basketball is who I am." He understands the difference. I didn't.

The coolest thing about that statement is: Kyrie's identity is not defined by basketball. That's impressive because a lot of times, the way that other people view us can affect the way we view ourselves.

Here's an example: Mike's one of the top basketball players in the country for his age. He's fifteen years old in the picture below:

Anytime he throws a picture up on Instagram, he's getting between 500–800 likes. Why are people interested in Mike? He gets a lot of attention because he's good at basketball.

Let's go deeper: Do you see how for some athletes their feelings of acceptance and belonging could be tied to their success in their sport?

Here's another example: Napheesa Collier put this up on her Instagram and look how many likes she got—close to 1,500.

Why is she getting that much attention? She's good at basketball. Do you see how it would be possible for Napheesa to misconstrue this attention as someone caring about her as a person, when in all actuality, they really just care about her as an athlete?

Mike, Napheesa, and I were having a conversation about this. I asked them to think about something. I asked them, "When people come up to you, do they ever ask you, 'How are you doing, Mike? How are you doing Napheesa?'"

They said, "No." What is everybody asking them? What college are you going to? Which AAU team do you play for? How's your season? All the questions they get are basketball-related questions.

The reason people know them and try to associate with them is because of how they perform at their sport. Almost everybody sees them as a player first and a person second. Do you see how it would be easy for them to create their identities based on these interactions with people as a player first, and a person second?

Note: If a coach views their players that way, then they are contributing to the way that their players see themselves. In my opinion, we have to get the order right. We have to have a multi-dimensional approach to grow the person first and the player second if we want to have a lasting, meaningful impact on the people that we work with.

Over 80% of the Time

To become the best player you can become, you have to go through a significant amount of adversity. Here's a great example of how a coach got a player to understand this point. The player was one of the top point guards in the country. The coach asked him three questions:

Coach: Would you be upset if you shoot less than fifty percent for the game?

The player says, "Yes."

Coach: Would you be upset if you have five or more turnovers?

The player says, "Yes."

Coach: OK, would you be upset if you lose?

The player says, "Yes."

You can see where he's coming from, right?

We did some research. We looked at the first three years in the NBA for Kyrie Irving. Here's how often one or more of those things happened to him during those first three years:

2011–2012 Season: 86% of the time
2012–2013 Season: 81% of the time
2013–2014 Season: 85% of the time

Think about that for a second. Kyrie is dealing with adversity over 80% of the time.

What'd Kyrie say? "Basketball is what I do." It's not who he is. Kyrie views himself as a person first. Player second. By him viewing himself that way, how did that help him deal with those difficult first three years?

Well, if he had viewed himself as a player first, he would have seen the situation as a threat and felt like a failure. But, because he views himself as a person first, those three years became an opportunity for him to build resilience and become a stronger person. Do you see the difference?

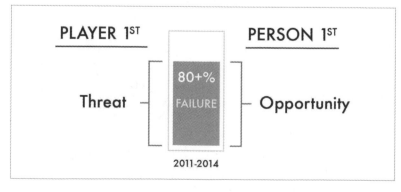

People who view themselves as Players First are <u>defined by their results</u> as a player. Which is why it's not "OK" for them to fail (their self-worth is attached to their performance).

People who view themselves as a Person First are <u>defined by how they handle results</u>, which are in their control. So, they handle success and failure in a much more stable way.

And it's important to note: If you view yourself as a person first, that does not mean that you don't chase excellence as hard as someone who views him or herself as a player first. You just value the outcome in a different way.

So the question becomes: How do you see yourself? Do you see yourself as a player first, or a person first?

When we realize that who we become as a result of the chase is the most important thing, we get the order right: Person First. Player Second.

And our sport then becomes a platform for us to show the world **who we are as a person.**

It's What I Live For

It was moments before tip-off. We were playing a top-10 team in the country. The arena was packed.

My assistant coach came up to me and asked, "Brett, you ready?"

I said, "I live for this."

Fast forward ten years later: I'm watching an interview on TV before a big game.

A reporter asks a player, "Are you ready for tonight's game?"

The player says, "This is what I live for."

His answer took me back to the place where I had been. I felt for him because I realized how dangerous that answer could be.

If that's what we live for—for big moments in our sport—and I'm guilty of this, it's a good indicator that we have a pretty shallow life. But, unfortunately, that's how society programs us.

Can I Get a Picture?

It's hard for NBA star Blake Griffin to walk around anywhere without getting asked, "Can I get a picture with you?"

Let's break this down. I'm going to ask you two questions.

First Question: Why do people want to take a picture with Blake Griffin? Is it because he's a great person, or is it because he's a great player? People want to get their picture with him because he's a great player.

People aren't saying, "Man, that guy is unselfish—I've got to get a picture with him." What are they thinking? They're thinking, "This guy dunks on everyone. Let me get a quick picture with him."

Second Question: Why would the person send (or post) that picture to all of their friends? One of our players said, "To get 'Likes' or 'Favorites.'" They're using Blake Griffin to show their friends how cool they are. In other words, they're increasing their social status by using Blake.

This is what happens to him (or anyone that's received a lot of recognition for what they do) all the time. And that's just a picture. Can you imagine what it's like in real life? One of the players that I work with is going through this. He said, "I don't feel like I've changed, but it feels like everyone around me has." That's a tough spot to be in.

The outside world values Blake Griffin for what he does. He's a basketball player. Do you see how it would be easy for him to think that's how he provides value? He learned a valuable lesson early in his pro career.

Identify Your Inner Circle

Blake Griffin went through a rough time his rookie year. He had a season-ending injury. When I talked with him about it, here's what he told me:

The attention you get from people…it can go away. My rookie year, when I got hurt and I wasn't able to play for a whole year, I saw that happen. People who used to talk to me going into the draft or going into my last year of college—I didn't hear from them.

There were people that were in my life, my friends and family, and those are the people that I realized are really with me. To this day, I'll never forget the people that really were there.

You kind of have to discern and be loyal to the people that are with you for who you are.

I love the last line. What does the word **discern** mean? Discern means to recognize. In other words, recognize and be loyal to the people that are with you for **who you are**.

After showing our players this, we ask them to draw a circle. We then ask them, "If you had a career-ending injury, who would still be there for you loving you and supporting you unconditionally?"

We then have them write down all of the names inside that circle. After they get done we ask, "Do you know what that is?"

They respond, "My inner circle."

The people that you write down in that circle are the people that view you as a person first. They are the people that have your best interest at heart. Take a second to write down who's in your inner circle.

Here's why it's important to insulate yourself with those people.

Identity Foreclosure

A championship coach asked his team, "Would you rather:"

1. Play in the NBA.
2. Have good character.

(Luckily, this isn't an either/or question—you can have both. The coach just wanted to see what was ultimately most important to his players.)

What do you think they said? 9 out of 11 guys said they'd pick, "Go to the NBA." Those numbers are consistent with the results that I get when I ask players that question. As you read this, there's a good chance you're thinking, "I'm picking playing professionally too."

Here's what's interesting: Playing in the NBA *is what you do*. Having good character is *who you are*. If you picked playing professionally—do you see how that shows that you value *what you do* over *who you are*?

I love asking the athletes that pick playing professionally: If you didn't play your sport, who would you be? When I ask them that question, I usually get an awkward silence because they haven't considered it.

There's a term for that. It's called identity foreclosure. Identity foreclosure happens when <u>what you do</u> becomes <u>who you are</u>. You lose your personal identity and you take on an athletic identity. In other words, your sport takes possession of who you are as a person. Your self-worth is then determined by your performance.

If you don't know who you are as a person, then why would character development be important? It wouldn't. Which is why athletes feel unfulfilled when they reach success. They're left with an empty feeling.

They then find ways to distract themselves from that reality. Maybe it's through sex, drinking, or drugs. Or by keeping so busy they don't have to look themselves in the mirror. Or by having people around them who are constantly telling them how good they are.

That's why it's critical for you to insulate your inner circle. The better you become at your sport, the more the outside world takes interest. Those forces become very strong and it becomes very easy to associate your self-worth with your athletic performance. If you can create a situation where the forces of your inner circle are stronger than the external forces, it can help you stay grounded in your identity as a person.

Abby Wambach learned a trick to help with this back when she was in high school. Abby is currently the all-time leading goal scorer for the USA women's national soccer team. Back when Abby was a senior in high school, she was the national player of the year.

I talked with her about having an athletic identity. She said, "In high school, I had a fake name that I would say because I was fairly well known in my little hometown of Rochester, New York. So my friends would call me Amy when I was out instead of Abby."

Abby's inner circle was concerned with who she was as a person versus who she was a soccer player.

Who's on Your Board of Directors?

Sue Enquist is a championship coach who was a part of eleven softball national championships at UCLA. One of the first things that she does with the high-level athletes (or coaches) that she works with is asks, "Who's on your board of directors?"

What's a board of directors? Many successful businesses have a board of directors. It's a collection of people that oversee the activities of a business and help provide different perspectives to help the business grow. Why not have a board of directors that could help you with what you do?

What's the difference between your inner circle and your board of directors? Your inner circle cares more about *who you are*. Your board of directors helps with *what you do*. You can have people that are in your inner circle who are on your board of directors. But, the purpose of your board is to create a go-to list of people that can help guide you with what you are doing.

I was talking with Abby Wambach about this idea and I asked her, "Do you like it?" She smiled enthusiastically and said, "I think it's a fantastic idea. I've never heard of it put in that specific way."

I told Blakely about the idea and she really liked it as well. She told me, "You're in charge of character development."

That's the perfect position for me with Blakely because here's the thing: I don't know much about soccer. I asked her, "What do you think of Abby being on your board?" She responded the way I thought she would and said, "She would be perfect."

She would be. Blakely is striving to be in a similar position as Abby. Abby has a lot of answers to the test that I could never give Blakely when it comes to the path she will be traveling. I asked Abby if she'd talk to Blakely—she responded, "Anytime."

When they talk Blakely is going to ask her to have a seat on the board. Take some time to consider, *who's on your board?* Here's one instance where it could have helped Blakely.

What Happens When Your Inner Circle Changes

As Blakely prepared for her first weekend playing college soccer, her parents had a simple message for her. They wanted to make sure that her expectations weren't too high.

Blakely had always received a lot of local attention for being a great scorer at the high-school level. The recognition she received didn't really affect her parents—they just wanted to see her have fun with the sport that she played. Her parents anticipated a tough transition from high school to major college athletics. Everybody close to her was prepared for a difficult transition.

As the first weekend approached for the player, both parents echoed the same message. They said, "Go have fun, enjoy the moment, and work hard."

That's exactly what Blakely did. In fact, that very first weekend, she surprised a lot of people. She had five goals in two games during her first weekend as a freshman.

Back home, her town was celebrating her success. The town took pride in the nationwide attention that she was receiving. Every member of her family enjoyed the attention that they were receiving as a result of her success. Her sister was even getting positive attention through social media channels each time she posted a picture of the two of them.

Do you see what happens? The status of everybody in Blakely's inner circle improved because of the affiliation they had with her.

When the parents experienced this, their message shifted.

Instead of saying, "Go have fun, enjoy the moment and work hard," the message turned into, "Let's get two goals this game." Or, "We need to take advantage of this lesser opponent."

I asked Blakely, "How has this affected you?"

She responded, "When I used to play bad I could feel like I could go home and escape from it. Nobody really cared that much about how I played—that made bad performances easier to get over.

Because they are receiving so much attention now from my play, it feels like they are experiencing my lows too. I feel like I don't have an escape from it all anymore."

That's a tough spot for Blakely to be in. The good news: success has put Abby Wambach in a bunch of tough situations. Abby can use her experiences to help Blakely understand how to manage the things with her family. This is a perfect example that shows how a board of directors can help you with your inner circle.

Here's another example.

How Quickly Things Change

As a sophomore in high school, Michael's team lost. It was the team's first loss of the season and everyone took it rough. The good news: they had a game the next day.

The next morning he decided that he was going to do something different. He woke up and at breakfast he decided that he was going to put his phone away for the day and not pay attention to social media. He put all of his energy into preparing for the game that evening.

That night things changed for Mike. Mike had an impressive dunk where he jumped from just inside the free-throw line and finished over someone. The crowd went wild. So did a video that a fan (who Mike didn't know) filmed.

After the game, the fan came up to Mike and said that he captured the dunk on his phone and he would send it to him. Mike didn't really think it was that great of a dunk at the time. Mike put the video on his Vine.

The next thing you know, ESPN direct messages Mike and asks for permission to use the video. Two hours later it was number one on SportsCenter's Top 10. The dunk went viral on social media. Mike was the center of the sports world for a moment.

The video had over four million views in the first twelve hours. His followers on Twitter tripled, and he gained even more traction on Instagram.

And just like that, Mike was back on social media.

Can you blame him? Everybody was talking about him. If everybody were talking about you (especially at fifteen years old), wouldn't you want to know what they were saying?

Do you see how strong those forces are?

Isn't it ironic that the day Michael decided to distance himself from social media, the forces of everybody around him became so strong that he couldn't do it? He admitted, "I'd try to put my phone down, but I wanted to check it."

I have a high level of empathy for athletes in this situation. All Mike did was make one great play; it was everyone around him that created the change.

What does change look like?

- Now, after basketball games, the players from the opposing school routinely wait outside of his locker room to take pictures with him.

- On social media, he gets direct messages from girls he's never met telling him how cute he is and that he should text them.

- A teacher from an opposing school told their class, "If anybody can bring me back Michael Porter's autograph you'll get extra credit."

So what do you tell a player in this situation?

Sophomore Dunks from Free-Throw Line

I started to think about something. If I were going to Google that video, what search terms would I use? I decided *Sophomore Dunks from Free-Throw Line*. A lot of results came up. That got me thinking. Then I had a conversation with Michael about it:

Me: If somebody were going to Google you without using your name—what would they search?

Mike: Top 10 Dunk.

Me: Is that how you want to be defined?

Mike: No.

Me: Have you allowed that one play to impact your life?

Mike: Yeah.

Have you ever heard the line: One play doesn't define you? A lot of coaches use this line when things go wrong. I think it's just as critical when things go right. I thought it was important for Mike to distance himself from that play and let it die. It's dangerous to give one play that much power—here's the other side of that:

The day after the dunk happened, there was another video that went viral for a much different reason. It was a nationally tele-vised college basketball game that was tied with three seconds left. The team inbounded the ball and shot a corner three. It was clear that the ball was going to come up short.

A player from the other team jumped to grab the ball thinking it was going to be an air ball. Unexpectedly, the ball grazed the rim. It changed the line of flight for the ball and it hit the player's hand and bounced in. The player was distraught be-cause that play gave the other team the win and he felt like he lost his team the game.

I showed Michael the clip. (I knew he had already seen it…I'll show you how I knew that in just a second.)

After Michael watched it, I showed him a tweet that somebody sent that player:

You single handedly lost me $2,500. Way to score for the other team. #Loser

He said, "That's messed up, man."

Then I said, "It's about to get personal."

The reason I knew Michael saw this play (before I showed him) is because he tweeted about it. His tweet read:

Yo…what was that dude from (university's name) thinking?

That's when it got uncomfortable.

Me: If that player read your tweet, do you think he would he take that positively or negatively?

Mike: Negatively.

Me: Is that how you want to use your platform?

Mike: No.

You could tell Michael got it and the conversation then shifted to: *How do you want to use your platform?*

He realized two things:

1. Distance yourself from good/bad plays. (Let them die.)
2. Use the newfound attention in a strong, positive way.

Do you see the value in having someone on your board of directors that can help you see situations in a different way?

Repurpose

When I ask players: Why do you play? I usually get two answers:

1. It's fun.
2. I love it.

For a lot of people, as they get older, it becomes more of a job than a sport. When it does, why continue to play the sport when it's not fun or when you no longer love it?

What makes it worth it to continue to invest an enormous amount of time and energy into the sport?

There are a lot of players that I work with who really struggle with this question.

It all comes down to purpose. What if you used all of the forces that your sport provides as a vehicle to develop as a person by helping you build character?

And what if building character got results?

I believe it does and here's how I get players to understand that.

What About Results?

Blakely plays soccer and I was curious. I said to her, "In basketball, the first two questions you're getting after a game is: 'Did you win?' And, 'How many points did you score?' Can you relate to that?"

She laughed. She pulled out her phone and showed me a text conversation that happened the previous day with one of her youth coaches. Here's how it went:

Coach: Win? Score?

Blakely: 3-0. We played great.

Coach: Did you score?

Blakely: No

Coach: What happened?

(Quick tip: if you ever want to be a coach, DO NOT do this.)

What signal is that coach sending her when he asks, "What happened?"

Do you think she felt judged? Of course she did. The coach is signaling to her that something is wrong because she didn't score. Is it any wonder why there would be a high level of anxiety?

I pulled out a note that she wrote me from a previous conversation that we had. Here's what she wrote down:

So it is really hard for me to not focus on results when, in all honesty, that is all everyone cares about. I definitely believe that it shouldn't be about the results and I cannot let that control me; however, it still just bothers me that even if I personally focus on myself and not the results, the rest of the world (media, fans, success) still gives everything to the one with the results. That is the hardest thing for me.

Can you relate to that?

That really resonated with me. As a senior in high school, I led the state of Missouri in scoring in basketball. That got a lot of attention.

One of my classmates would bring a poster board to the game with a sharpie. He kept a tally of how many points I scored so the student body could keep track. So *I totally get* that results are all people care about.

Here's what I did with Blakely:

I gave her this list of these character skills and I asked her to pick three performance skills that she'd like to work on. And three moral skills that she'd like to work on.

CHARACTER SKILLS

PERFORMANCE		MORAL	
Hardworking	Resilient	Unselfish	Loyal
Competitive	Confident	Honest	Trustworthy
Positive	Enthusiastic	Respectful	Encouraging
Focused	Disciplined	Appreciative	Socially Aware
Accountable	Motivated	Humble	Caring
Courageous	Creative	Patient	Empathetic

Since the original character study that we conducted, we've expanded our list of character skills.

She picked Positive, Focused, and Resilient for her performance skills. She picked Unselfish, Appreciative, and Loyal for her moral skills.

I asked her four questions (and I'd like you to answer these questions too):

Me: Do you think that it's in your control to practice and improve these skills?

Blakely: Yes.

Me: OK. Do you think that if you became more Positive, Focused, and Resilient that it would actually make you a better player?

Blakely: Yes.

Me: Do you think that if you became more Unselfish, Appreciative, and Loyal that it would actually make you a better teammate?

Blakely: Yes.

Me: Do you see how, if you grew these skills, it would actually make you a better player and a better teammate, which would lead to better results?

Blakely: That makes complete sense.

Those four questions prove that by focusing on growing our character skills our performance will actually improve. Do you see that? So, instead of focusing on the result, we can shift our attention back to what drives the result and become a better person and player in the process.

3

Getting Ahead
of The Conversation

How Is He?

As we've covered, Michael gets a lot of attention as a basketball player. To the point where Michael's teammates are known as just that—*Michael's teammates*. After people ask his teammates, "You play with Michael?" What do you think the next question they get asked is? "How is he?"

How Michael's teammates answer that question is how they will remember him. That's the message that his teammates will then take into future conversations when they tell people, "I played basketball with Michael when he was in high school."

Your teammates are around you every day and get to see who you are as a person. When you're around someone that much—it's no longer about athletic achievement. It becomes about how you interact with them on a daily basis.

To that prove this point, I was talking with a college female athlete about this. She said, "I'm not going to invite someone to my wedding because they were an All-American."

Michael smiled at that point. We wanted to get ahead of the conversation that his teammates were going to have about him.

 Glossary

I start by getting the players (and teams) that I work with to understand why it's so important to have a glossary. I ask a few questions to illustrate the importance:

Me: Do you want to be positive?

They all say, "Yes."

I'll then ask, "How would you define the word positive?"

Get ready for an awkward pause. They usually need time to think about it.

Why don't you take a second to think about that? How would you define it?

If we do this at our Academy, we divide the players into five small groups. We then go around the room to see what they come up with. You know what's interesting? We'll have five different answers. 5 groups = 5 answers. Here are some of the most common answers we get:

- Happy
- Energetic
- Cheerful
- Motivated
- Optimistic

Think about this for a second. Let's look at the above examples.

What if the definition that we're working with for positive was "happy" or "cheerful?"

Put yourself in this situation: You've just missed six straight shots in the first half–can you be happy or cheerful in that moment? That's a conflict of interest, right? What would your teammates think if they saw you happy or cheerful while you were performing badly? That wouldn't work well, would it?

We created a glossary of simple and straightforward definitions of all of the character skills. (We'll cover how we define Positive shortly.)

Why Is Using a Glossary Important?

I want to go on record and say that I don't know anything about rugby. I do know that Jack Clark is a great rugby coach. He's won over twenty national championships at the University of California, Berkeley.

I asked him, "Why is using a glossary so important?"

Jack said, "We have a tendency to use phrases and words that if you ask ten different players, 'What does that mean?' They would all respond differently. But they'd say the right stuff differently. And, I don't know, if that's efficient? It's certainly not in the real-time of competition."

Same Station

When I'm working with players (or a team), I'll ask them to get their phones out. I'll then ask them to go through their music and pick their favorite song out. After they pick it, we all play our phones together. It sounds terrible.

The last time I did this, there was folk, rock, and hip-hop all mixed together. You can imagine how that sounded. It wasn't good.

After we do that, we say, "Alright, now we all have to find a song that we like." Depending on how similar your backgrounds are, this could take a while.

Sometimes, there might be an example where there are no songs that overlap from anybody's library. (In that case we use an invisible "iTunes gift card" and pick a song…together.)

Once we've come together and have the same song, we talk.

I'll ask them, "What was the point of that?"

One of my favorite answers came from a volleyball player who said, "When you are on a different station, you don't play as well together. But when you are both on the same station, you play better together."

She nailed it. That's exactly what a glossary does. It closes the communication gap and allows everybody involved to work from the same definition. Here's the glossary (and definitions) that we use with the players that we work with:

GLOSSARY

PERFORMANCE SKILLS

Hardworking: Paying the price with effort.

Competitive: Striving to be your best.

Positive: Good and useful thinking.

Focused: Eliminating distractions.

Accountable: Taking responsibility for your actions.

Courageous: Operating outside of your comfort zone.

Resilient: Bouncing back from setbacks.

Confident: Self-trusting.

Enthusiastic: Expressing enjoyment.

Disciplined: Self-regulating.

Motivated: Having a strong purpose.

Creative: Out-of-the-box thinking.

Curious: Desiring to learn or understand.

GLOSSARY

MORAL SKILLS

Unselfish: Putting the team first.

Honest: Telling the truth.

Respectful: Showing consideration.

Appreciative: Recognizing the good in someone or something.

Humble: Distributing credit.

Patient: Tolerating delay or struggle.

Loyal: Showing allegiance.

Trustworthy: Being reliable.

Trustwilling: Relying on others.

Encouraging: Giving confidence and support.

Socially Aware: Understanding signals sent and received.

Caring: Investing in the person.

Empathetic: Sharing the feelings of others.

Pick Your Character Skills

There are very few athletes that I come across who don't want to become a better person through their sport. The question then becomes: How do we make that happen? How do we actually use the sport that we love to become a better person?

Here's what I do with the players that I work with. I give them a character checklist with a bunch of performance and moral character skills on it. We then ask them to check off the top 5 performance skills and the top 5 moral skills that they would like to be known for.

CHARACTER CHECKLIST

PERFORMANCE	MORAL
☐ Hardworking	☐ Unselfish
☐ Competitive	☐ Honest
☐ Positive	☐ Respectful
☐ Focused	☐ Appreciative
☐ Accountable	☐ Humble
☐ Courageous	☐ Patient
☐ Resilient	☐ Loyal
☐ Confident	☐ Trustworthy
☐ Enthusiastic	☐ Trustwilling
☐ Disciplined	☐ Encouraging
☐ Motivated	☐ Socially Aware
☐ Creative	☐ Caring
☐ Curious	☐ Empathetic

They can be skills that they're already good at. They can be skills that they need to work on. But they are the skills they want to be known for **as a person**.

Here's an example of Michael's:

PERFORMANCE	MORAL
✔ Hardworking	✔ Honest
✔ Positive	✔ Respectful
✔ Focused	✔ Humble
✔ Disciplined	✔ Loyal
✔ Motivated	✔ Caring

Napheesa also completed a checklist:

PERFORMANCE	MORAL
✔ Hardworking	✔ Honest
✔ Competitive	✔ Appreciative
✔ Accountable	✔ Humble
✔ Confident	✔ Socially Aware
✔ Enthusiastic	✔ Caring

Write Your End-of-the-Year Banquet Speech

After our players pick the skills that they want to be known for, here's what we do:

We tell them that they are writing a story, and we have them write the final chapter of their story for the current year. We ask them to fast-forward to the end-of-the-year team awards banquet.

We ask them to pretend that either their coach or a teammate is getting up to address the room full of people—about them.

We ask, "What do you want them to say about you?" We actually have them write out the speech that they would want their coaches or teammates to say.

Here's the catch. They have to find a way to incorporate the ten skills that they checked off on their character checklist into their speech.

Here is Michael's speech:

*Michael…He's one of the most **positive** people I know. He always brings his best and is the most **hardworking** and **focused** (out of everyone) on our team. He doesn't need anyone to **motivate** him because he's one of the most **disciplined** guys I know. Mike is very **honest** with us. But at the same time, he's **caring** and **respectful**. Whenever we have a problem outside of basketball, we know he will be there for us because he's **loyal**. His **humility** is without question as well. Overall, he's just a great teammate and person.*

Here's an example of Napheesa's:

*Napheesa is an amazing person on and off the court. During practice she continues to be the **hardest working** person there. Her **competitiveness** helps to push her teammates to be better players. She is a **confident** leader, always holding herself and others **accountable**. And her **enthusiastic** spirit never dulls, even in tough or stressful situations. Napheesa is also the most **humble** person I know. She is **appreciative** towards everyone, and shows she **cares** for others by always being **socially aware**. She is also very **honest** and will give help to anyone who needs it. She was motivated to grow as person and help others every day. I can truly say that she was a joy having on the team.*

Isn't that awesome? We believe that who you become as a result of the chase is the most important thing. Once our players have their awards speech written, they have a road map for who they want to become. We then work to develop these things through the strong forces that the sport they love provides.

Important: I pick the character skills that I want to work on as their coach and I write my end-of-the-year speech. My speech is based around what I'd like them to say about me. I show it to them—that way, both parties understand who the other person is striving to become.

 ## Accountability Program

All of this is great, but how do we do it? How do we actually make it to where we're developing in an intentional way?

One thing that's really important to us is for our players to take accountability for their own development. Here's what it means to us:

Accountability: taking responsibility for your actions.

Here's how we weave accountability into our growth cycle. There are three stages to your growth:

Stage 1: Preparation

At the beginning of each week, I meet with Napheesa. We have a film session where we feature a character skill. We then use the rest of that day to come up with a plan for the week to help her take accountability for her development as a person. Here's how we do that. I ask her to pick one performance skill and one moral skill that she's going to focus on for the week based on her character checklist.

Performance Skill: Hardworking
Moral Skill: Appreciative

Once we've identified what she wants to work on, she writes on a notecard how she's going to do that. Here's an example of how we would work on the performance skill Hardworking:

Make 150 shots before practice 3x this week.

Here's an example of how she can work on the moral skill Appreciative:

Write three thank-you notes to teammates.

After she identifies what she's going to work on, she gives me the card.

(Just a reminder: I am not telling her what to write on her card. It's her idea. She's taking accountability for her own development.)

Stage 2: Performance

Here's the deal: for every day I see a player, they spend six days on their own. Those six days are critical for their development. How they execute their plan will determine the amount of growth that happens. (Side note: Discipline is critical in the performance stage. This is where self-regulation occurs.)

Stage 3: Reflection

We start off each weekly meeting with a question. I ask her, "Do you get your card back?"

If she completed the tasks on her card from the previous week, she gets her card back. If she doesn't, I keep it. Over the course of the season, we keep track of how many of her cards she gets back.

We've created a situation where she has to confront herself and take responsibility for her actions. That's why we call the notecards Accountability Cards.

Conclusion: Your Road Map

What should you take away from Part I? My hope is that you learn to separate yourself as a person from yourself as an athlete. I hope that you understand that by developing and strengthening your character, you will actually become a better player, which will then lead to better results. We've learned that character drives the process, which drives the result.

Start Here:

1. What's Holding You Back?
Identify what's holding you back and isolate the five things that you struggle with most.

2. Write a Letter to Your Sport.
Explain to your sport (as if it were a person) how it's holding you back. Incorporate the five things that you struggle with most.

3. Identify Your Inner Circle.
Who would still support and love you unconditionally if you had a season-ending injury? Surround yourself with people that view you as a person first to combat having your identity defined exclusively by your athletic performance.

4. Build Your Board of Directors.
This is a list of go-to people that can help you with what you do. You can have people from your inner circle on your board—but this group of people helps guide you on your path.

5. Use a Glossary.

Before picking the character skills that you want to focus on, make sure that you can clearly define each skill. We invite you to use our glossary, or you can create your own before deciding what skills you want to focus on.

6. Pick 5 Performance and 5 Moral Skills.

Identify the skills that you want to build and be known for during the upcoming year.

7. Write Your End-Of-The-Year Awards Banquet Speech.

Get ahead of the conversation. Write out what you want your team and coaches to say about you so it gives you a vision of who you are striving to become.

8. Use An Accountability Program.

Take accountability for your character development on a weekly basis. Ask somebody on your board of directors to use our notecard system to help make sure you are becoming the person you want to be on your chase.

PART II

A chronicle of my time with a player named
Kenny and his development as a person

The very first question I asked Kenny was "Do you love your sport?"

He responded, "Yes."

I then asked, "Why don't you love it when you play it?"

He smiled and said, "That's a good question."

Kenny has always been driven to succeed. Nothing was going to stop him from chasing excellence. The problem: the pressure was stealing away the fun for him.

I asked him, "If I would have met you when you were thirteen years old and I would have told you that you would be in the exact position you are in right now (he's the best player on a really good team), would that make you happy?

Kenny responded, "Yes."

Me: Are you happy?

Kenny: No.

Me: Why not?

Kenny: (Silence) I don't know.

Me: Can I help you?

Kenny: Yes.

The first thing that I did with Kenny was I helped him under-stand the difference between "Kenny <u>The Player</u>" and "Kenny <u>The Person</u>." We needed to get him to distance himself from his sport to reflect on the relationship that he had with it. Kenny and I started to talk about the things that were holding him back.

To help him better understand his relationship with his sport, I asked Kenny to write a letter to his sport as if it were a person. I wanted him to explain why it's taking him away from the person that he wants to be. (He incorporated the five things he struggled with the most from the "What's Holding You Back?" sheet.)

Dear Basketball,

I think I've lost myself in what I can achieve with you. I'm not really sure who I would be without you. We've had a lot of success together and you've brought me a lot of attention. Do you remember when we would spend time alone together? I used to lose track of time when I was with you.

Now, I feel a lot of pressure to succeed. People are starting to expect more and more from me and I don't want to fail for all of the people that have helped me. I've started to hear a lot of outside criticism—it's hard to stay positive and it drives me to want to be perfect. I'm con-stantly measuring myself up against others who spend time with you because I want to be the best.

You have come between my relationships with others. My friends think that I choose you over them. They're probably right. It's because I want to make it so bad, which is why I struggle with the relationships I have with my teammates. They think that I'm selfish but I feel like they don't care about being great as much as I do. Both are probably true. I know that I could show them that I do care about them I just get so caught up in doing my thing.

I guess I'm scared that you will hurt me. What if I look back and I invest all of this time in you and I don't make it? Will it all have been a waste of time when I could have been exploring other options?

-Kenny

I asked Kenny, "You spend a lot of time with your sport, right?"

Kenny nodded his head and responded, "A lot."

Me: You feel like you've made a lot of sacrifices for this, right?

Kenny: Man. All of my friends have time to hang out—I don't. Sometimes I question if it's worth it.

Me: What if we repurposed all of that time? What if we used all of the forces of sport to help you develop you as a person? Do you see how that can help you past your career as an athlete? Then you won't feel like you're wasting your time regardless of what happens.

He smiled and said, "That sounds great. But how do I do that?"

After we went through who was in his inner circle and who was on his board of directors (he asked me to be his director of character development), I handed Kenny a character checklist along with a glossary of simplified definitions. I asked him to pick out five performance skills and five moral skills. Here's what he picked:

PERFORMANCE	MORAL
☑ Positive	☑ Unselfish
☑ Confident	☑ Encouraging
☑ Courageous	☑ Appreciative
☑ Resilient	☑ Trustworthy
☑ Competitive	☑ Caring

I asked Kenny, "Do you think that if we work together, we could improve all of these skills?"

Kenny: Yeah.

Me: If you improved these performance skills would that make you a better player?

Kenny: Yeah.

Me: If you improved these moral skills would that make you a better teammate and a better friend?

Kenny: Yes.

Me: Here's what we're going to do. I want you to fast forward to your team's end-of-the-year awards banquet. I'd like you to script out what you would want your teammates or coaches to say about you in a speech. I'd like you to weave all of the ten skills that you picked into the speech. Sound good?

Kenny: (Smiling) Yep.

Here's what Kenny wrote:

*Kenny made me better. He was **unselfish** in a way that he always put the team first. That takes **courage**—he did the right thing even when it was the hardest. I always admired his ability to be **encouraging**. He did it in a way that made you want to be better because you knew that he **cared** about you as a person. He **appreciated** everybody on the team.*

*I can't remember a day where he came in and he wasn't **positive**. His **competitive** spirit pushed all of us to be better. I admired his ability to not let mistakes bother him. He was **resilient**. The **confidence** he had inside himself spilled over to us.*

*I think because we saw all of these things happen on a daily basis everybody viewed him as **trustworthy**. There's no doubt in my mind that I am a better player and person because I was on the same team as Kenny.*

When Kenny finished writing his speech, I asked him, "How important is it for your teammates to think this of you?"

Kenny responded, "It's real important."

Me: Can we explore what each of these skills look like?

Kenny: Let's do it.

PERFORMANCE

- ☑ Positive
- ☑ Confident
- ☑ Courageous
- ☑ Resilient
- ☑ Competitive

☑ Positive

We started with the character skill Positive. I asked, "Do you beat yourself up when you make mistakes?

Kenny: (Smiling) I struggle with that.

Me: When you're talking negatively to yourself—not only is the competitor making it difficult on you but who else is?

Kenny: Me.

Me: Do you see the energy that you're wasting?

Kenny: How do I change that?

Me: We're going to start by looking at what golf can teach us.

What Golf Can Teach Us

College golf can teach us a great lesson. I was working with a high-level college team and I asked the team a few questions:

Me: How long does it take for you to complete a swing?

Team: One second.

Me: How many shots will you take in a normal round?

Team: 72.

Me: How long does a normal round take to play?

Team: 5 hours.

Me: Let me get this straight, you're only swinging a golf club for one minute and twelve seconds out of 300 minutes?

Think about that for a second. The great golfers are the ones who can manage the other two hundred, ninety-eight minutes, and forty-eight seconds the best.

I asked them a few more questions:

Me: Out of the 72 shots, how many go exactly according to plan (outside of tap-ins)?

Team: (Laughing) 5–10.

In college, players caddy their own bags. Five players play and only two coaches are present. What does that mean? Players spend a lot of time by themselves, between shots, when (most of the time) things aren't going according to plan.

Nobody on the team had ever really thought about it like that before. How we manage the time in-between shots is critical, and having strong positive thoughts is critical.

Your Two Voices

We have two voices—a public voice and a private voice. Think of it this way:

Public voice: This is your voice that everybody gets to hear. It's what you say out loud. A lot of times this is the "edited version" of what you are thinking.

Private voice: This is your voice that only you have access to. These are your innermost thoughts. It's the "uncut version" of how you process a situation.

Jim Loehr talked to me about the private voice. Here are two questions that he asks his players to consider:

1. How does it speak to you?
2. Is it someone who helps you out or breaks you down?

He added, "Once you realize that, that voice is almost always saying something, you can start to take responsibility for how that voice is actually speaking to you. This voice will be the only voice that's with you until your death. You want it to be somebody who's a contributor to your life."

Here's how we illustrate this point to our Academy.

The Scrolling Scoreboard

Put yourself in this situation: you're in a game. The whole student body is watching you. Things are going badly for you. Things are going badly for your team. You are losing 28–42 to a team that you should be beating.

What if the thoughts that you were thinking in that moment scrolled across the bottom of the scoreboard for the entire gym to see? How would you feel?

I love asking that question to players because they start to laugh. They know they'd be embarrassed. They wouldn't want people to see the way they talk to themselves.

One person said, "My friends have never heard me talk like that."

Can you relate?

Think about this: when you talk negatively to yourself, not only are you being challenged by the other team, but you're also making it harder on yourself. Think about the energy that you're wasting.

We need to win the conversation in our head. We need to turn our private voice into an inner coach that can guide us through the storms of life. Building a player's inner coach is one of the most important things that we do.

Brad Stevens

What does a good inner coach look like in real life? There's an example that we show every player that we work with that has become the gold standard for what our inner coach should look like.

Here's the situation: Butler is down one against Gonzaga with 4.6 seconds left. They have the ball and have to take it the length of the floor. They inbound it to their point guard and he travels, giving the ball back to Gonzaga—up one with 3 seconds left.

If you're Butler and that happens, 99% of the time you lose that game. As soon as the point guard is called for traveling, if you pay attention to Brad Stevens, the head coach of Butler at the time, he calmly walks to his bench and subs a player in for the next play. (Important to note: he didn't sub out the player who made the mistake.)

Gonzaga gets ready to inbound the ball and has trouble. As the ball is inbounded it's deflected and Butler steals it. Their player takes it the length of the court and makes a game-winning floater as the buzzer sounds. Pandemonium ensues. It was magic and everybody in Hinkle Fieldhouse went crazy… except for one person.

If you zoom in on Brad Stevens, and you keep your eye on him the entire time, you'll notice that his demeanor doesn't change at all from his observant (arms crossed) posture. As the ball goes in, and he's surrounded by chaos, he calmly walks down to shake the other coach's hand.

Why is this one of my favorite clips of all time? You have two plays to end the game. One play is an example of extreme failure. The other is an example of extreme success. His reaction to each is identical.

That's what a strong inner coach looks like. A strong inner coach has the ability to counterbalance the external forces and sift through that chaos in order to get you to the next step despite what's going. That's what Positive looks like to us. Here's how we define the word:

Positive: good and useful thinking.

Creating Awareness for Change

There are times when you have to create awareness for players in order for them to understand that they need to change their behavior. Such is the case with Brandon. Brandon is a Division I player in his sport.

When I went to watch him play, I noticed something. I noticed how poor his body language was. It was a clear indicator of his thought processes and it was obvious that he was getting in his own way. We needed to change that.

During a tournament championship game I had three younger players, three peers, and three parents watch Brandon and write down their observations. I asked them, "If somebody asked you about him and you had to sum him up in one word, what would your word be?"

Here's some of the feedback that I got:

Parents:	Peers:	Younger players:
"Difficult."	"Negative."	"Mad."
"Frustrated."	"Cocky."	"Moody."
"Entitled."	"Superior."	"Selfish."

I brought Brandon in and I asked him, "Would you like me to help you?"

He said, "Yes."

I explained to him what I did and I gave him the stack of cards with the feedback facing down so he couldn't see what was on them. Each card had one response (from above) on it. He sat across from me and held the stack of nine cards up with the answers facing in my direction. I held up a mirror and he looked in the mirror and read each one of the cards.

After we finished reading through the deck of cards, I asked him what the point of that exercise was. He got pretty emotional. I told him that it was my job to help him see himself the way that other people see him (hence the mirror). Sometimes it's difficult to be aware of the story that you are unknowingly telling others.

I asked him, "Is this the story that you want to tell?"

He said, "No."

Me: You have an opportunity. You can take this feedback and use it to make you better, or you can dismiss it.

Brandon: I want to use it.

Me: Do you want my help to change it?

Brandon: Yes.

Me: It's going to be really hard.

Brandon: I'm ready.

We celebrated that he took accountability for his actions. He owned his actions and accepted the challenge of changing his behavior for the future. We were off to a great start.

I gave Brandon five tools to help him out with becoming more positive. The first tool we explored: best friend advice. I shared a story with Brandon to show him how to use it.

Tool: Best Friend Advice

I was working with a player who tore her ACL during the summer entering her senior year. The day she found out that she was going to have to miss half of her senior season, we met up. She was devastated.

Me: I know I'm supposed to feel bad. And I do. But I don't think that's what you need right now.

Player: (Starts laughing)

Me: Here's what we are going to do. I want you to pretend that your best friend is in the exact same situation that you are. What advice would you give her?

I typed out her advice as she recited it to me:

There's a good chance that you will be able to play—the year isn't going to be completely gone. It's good that you are getting your surgery next week so you can start the process faster. It's great that your family and friends are being really supportive. And you're still going to have a role on the team even though you aren't going to get to play.

I know that you are afraid of feeling left out because you won't actually be on the court. I know that you are afraid that you won't be able to come back at the level that you were at. I know that you are afraid that you will lack the patience and want to skip steps. You probably are thinking, "What am I going to do with my time?"

You are going to physical therapy tomorrow—focus on that. You are going to talk with people who have already had ACL surgery and getting their advice on how to deal with everything will help you understand what you should expect after the surgery.

Every time I'm in these situations with athletes, I'm amazed. I'm amazed at what happens when people go inside themselves for answers. It makes me smile because (most of the time) they give themselves better advice than I could have ever given them. This is where their self-discovery often occurs because they never realized the power of their own inner coach.

For whatever reason, a lot of players don't look to their inner coach to get answers. After we get done with that exercise, I'll ask players, "Why don't you rely on your inner coach more?"

One player reflected and sent me this:

When I was talking to you today my mind was going and without even realizing it, my inner coach was fully engaged. Now, I just need to continue practicing that. I normally know what to say, like when you tell me to coach you. Now, I just need to get my inner coach to coach me.

How do we build anything? We build skill by practicing. The more we can go inside for advice, the more we discover about our ability to coach ourselves.

The Action between the Action

Do you remember how long a golfer is actually swinging? One minute and twelve seconds out of 300 minutes. Managing the time in-between action is critical. The person that helped me realize that there was a game within a game was Jim Loehr.

Tennis (like a lot of sports) is interesting because you spend much more time in-between action than you do actually playing the sport. What happens with all of that time between points? What is going on? Jim Loehr has worked with the best players in the world. He focuses on coaching the "down time" just as much as he does the action.

He had a player who struggled with being positive (good and useful thinking).

Here's what he did: he had the player wear headphones in a practice match. Jim sat in the bleachers. As they played, Jim would talk into a microphone in-between points. The player could actually hear what Jim was saying to him through the headphones. Jim would say the thoughts that he wanted the player to be thinking in that moment.

What's Jim doing? He's giving his player a model for what a productive inner coach looks like in-between points. In other words, he's coaching the game within the game. The action between the action. How can you coach yourself (in your sport) in-between the action of the game?

Tool: Plan Positive

Here's what I do to help change the inner dialogue of the players that I work with. I call it Plan Positive. What's the word plan mean?

Plan: to decide ahead of time.

Plan Positive means: to decide ahead of time how to have good and useful thinking.

In other words it's a planned performance. You develop a set of habits and thought processes (before a situation happens) to help you handle a situation better when you're actually going through it.

Here are the two most important elements of Plan Positive:

1. Content: what you want to say to yourself.
2. Tone: how you want to say it.

We have Plan Positive Cards that look like this:

How It Works

Identify a situation that you know you don't handle very well. The question I love asking is: What is something that your teammates or coaches do to push your buttons?

Write that under "Tough Situation."

Example: coach yells at me for my mistakes.

Develop the content that you want your inner coach to say the next time you're in that situation. You are preparing yourself for the situation so when you are in it, you just follow the habits and things don't spiral.

Example: take the information that the coach is saying and disregard the tone.

Your tone is critical. Think about it like this: Imagine making a major mistake, how are you talking to yourself?

I asked a player, "What if you talked to your friends in the tone that you talk to yourself?"

The player responded, "I wouldn't have any friends."

We give our players a bank of tones to choose from to help guide their thoughts on what's most useful for them:

1. Encouraging
2. Confident
3. Informative
4. Supportive
5. Patient

Example: in the scenario of the coach yelling at me, I'd pick an encouraging tone to help reassure me.

Tool: Replace Negative

One of the most common questions that I get asked is: "How do I get back to being positive once I go negative?"

There are three steps that we've found to be helpful.

First Step: Acknowledge the Thought

Don't judge your thought—that is unproductive. What does it mean when you acknowledge something? You become aware or recognize it. Once you acknowledge the thought is negative, what do you do?

Second Step: Interrupt the Thought

What does the word interrupt mean? It means to stop. When you interrupt a thought, you cut it off. After you've cut the thought off you can replace it.

Third Step: Replace the Thought

When you replace something, what do you do? You exchange it. You can replace your negative thought with a **good and useful** thought.

Think back to the scoreboard example. When you make a mistake and things aren't going your way—what are you thinking? The key is to be able to recognize when you are having negative thoughts in the moment.

For example: your coach takes you out after making a mistake. Let's say you are thinking to yourself, "Are you serious right now? Why do I even play this sport?" Is that productive? Obviously not, right? So here's how it works:

1. Acknowledge the thought: "Are you serious right now? Why do I even bother playing?"
2. Interrupt the thought.
3. Replace the thought: "Encourage my teammate who's coming in for me."

Here's another tool that compliments the Replace Negative tool well. It's called the Opportunity Converter.

Tool: Opportunity Converter

Why do we go negative? It happens when we allow the external (outside things) to dictate the way we feel internally. It goes against human nature to be positive when the situations you are in aren't favorable.

What if there's a way to change that? What if it came down to a mind shift that would guarantee that you would be fueled by positive energy?

Here's a strategy that effectively replaces negative thoughts with good and useful thoughts: convert everything into an opportunity for growth.

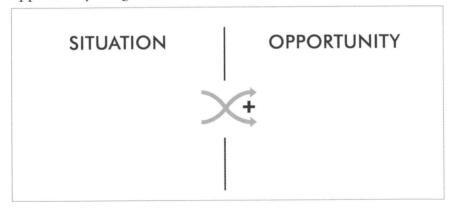

When you do this, you're forcing yourself to operate on the good and useful side of the equation. Everything comes down to how you frame the moment. (A lot of players try to think of it as a game–they want to get better at reframing the moment into an opportunity.)

Here are a few examples:

If somebody's late It's an opportunity to build patience

If your teammate misses a game-winning opportunity It's an opportunity to be encouraging

If you have to get up at 5:30 a.m. for a workout It's an opportunity to build discipline

It takes work. It takes practice. But when you repurpose moments where you could "go negative" into opportunities for personal growth, you are taking full advantage of the moment. That's what "good and useful" thinking looks like.

Tool: Don Meyer Notebook

Here's when I knew a player got it. She came up short in a game-winning situation and her team lost a critical game. After the game, the player told me, "I can beat myself up for twenty minutes or for two days. Either way, I'm getting to the same place. Why not get to that spot sooner so I have an extra two days to prepare for the next thing?"

That's great logic, isn't it?

Why don't we do that? I ask players that question all the time. Some say, "I feel like if I move on too quick, my teammates and coaches won't think that I care." Can you relate to that? Think about that for a second. How backwards is that? Do you see how when you do that, you're wasting energy?

After we cover that point, I'll ask players, "After games, do you remember the good things you did? Or the bad things?" They all respond, "The bad things." Do you have trouble with getting over bad performances?

If so, here's a great tool that Hall-of-Fame coach Don Meyer did with his team. Don had his players write down in their notebooks the answer to two questions:

What did I do well **and why**?

What can I do better **and how**?

The end of each section is bold because it's an action item. It directs your attention to the future to help you get over a bad performance and move in the right direction.

What did I do well **and why**? The why creates a repeat button. In other words, the next time you are in the same situation, you'll know what to do.

What can I do better **and how**? This forces you to move past the mistake. It takes your focus from what happened to how you are going to create a plan to prevent it from happening again.

My suggestion: the next time you are in a situation where you are having a tough time moving on, get with a coach (or do it individually) and answer these two questions. That will put you in a place where you are directing your energy toward future progress. That's what good and useful thinking looks like.

5 Ways to Exercise Positivity

1. **Give Your Best Friend Advice:**
   Not literally, but pretend that they are going through the situation that you are struggling with. Write down the advice that you would give them. And then take it.

2. **Plan Positive:**
   Identify a future situation that you know you'll be in and create the content (what you want to say) and the tone (how you want to say it) to help your inner coach's dialogue.

3. **Replace Negative:**
   Pay attention to your thought processes. How do you reset? Once you are aware of a negative thought, interrupt it. Then replace it with good and useful thinking.

4. **Opportunity Converter:**
   Find ways to repurpose negative situations (and positive situations) into an opportunity to grow.

5. **Don Meyer Notebook:**
   Turn results into guideposts. To help you move past a situation, ask yourself: "What did I do well and why?" And, "What can I do better and how?"

☑ Confidence

I asked Kenny, "Is your confidence attached to the result? Meaning, if you play well, you feel more confident? And if you play poorly, you feel less confident?"

He said, "Yes."

Me: Would you agree that those results are not fully within your control?

Kenny: Yes.

Me: Are you open to learning about attaching your confidence to something that is within your control?

Kenny: Yes.

Me: Here's a conversation I had with an athlete that I was working with.

Confidence and Control

I was having a conversation with a high-level athlete. He dominates his sport in high school. I asked him a few questions about his confidence.

Me: Do you agree that you feel most confident when you feel like you are in control?

Player: Yes.

Me: Because you're so good at your sport, you have a lot of control when it comes to the outcome of the game. What if you're in situations where you don't feel like you're in control? Are you confident then?

Player: No.

Me: I think a lot of athletes hide behind their talent. But when it comes down to it, they're insecure—do you agree?

Player: That's me, man.

First off, when you are good at something and everybody recognizes that, it becomes challenging to admit that you aren't confident *because of your image*. Which is why this next conversation I had with a player is so important.

I asked him, "Why does the attention matter to you so much?"

He responded, "It never did until I got it and then it was gone."

Me: Is your confidence attached to that attention?

Player: Yes.

A lot of people attach their confidence to things outside of themselves (like attention). Can we control anything outside of us? No. For this player, when he didn't get the attention, what happened? He questioned his ability. He is anchoring his confidence and the way he feels about himself to something external that's not in his control. Do you see that?

Three Questions For You

How would you answer these three questions:

1. What's your definition of confidence?
2. How do you build confidence?
3. Why do people struggle with confidence?

I ask these three questions to players and coaches and it's amazing how similar the answers I get are. Here are the most common answers that I get:

Question #1: What is the definition of confidence?
"Believing in yourself."

Question #2: How do you build it?
"Having success."
"Preparation."
"The people around you."

Question #3: Why do people struggle with confidence?
"Expectations of others."
"Failing."
"Criticism."
"Comparisons to others."

What do all of the reasons that people struggle with confidence have in common? They all contribute to the enemy of confidence: self-doubt.

A Few Thoughts

I was talking with a player and I asked him, "How would you define confidence?"

He responded, "Believing in yourself."

Me: Believing in yourself to do what?

Player: Accomplish a goal.

Me: So you build confidence through success?

Player: Confidence is built by setting a goal and achieving it.

Do you remember the first part of the book? What did we establish about goals? Result-based goals aren't fully within our control. If we feel most confident when we are in control, do you see how there's a conflict?

What if we shifted the way we viewed confidence? Let's start by redefining the word.

Defining Confidence

I believe there has to be a different way of thinking about confidence—a way that is within our control. We've been working for a while to establish a definition that can be accessed in all situations.

The enemy of confidence is: self-doubt. We define the word confidence as the opposite: self-trust.

Confidence: Self-trust

How do we define trust? To rely on someone or something.

Self-trust means that you rely on yourself.

How's that different from how you viewed it before? Before, what was our confidence attached to? It was attached to an outcome—an external outcome that isn't within our control. Now we are attaching our confidence to something internal—that's within our control.

Important: Confidence (self-trust) can be built by tying it to an external source such as achievement—it's just not as stable because it's not fully within our control. Internal confidence (self-trust) is a sustainable confidence that can be applied across all situations because it's attached to things within our control. It's trusting in your ability to handle the moment (regardless of the outcome) and external sources provide the moment.

What Confidence Looks Like

Situation: you're playing the #2 ranked basketball team in the country. You are having an off game, you're 0–5 from the three-point line. What if your coach drew up a play for you to take the game-tying three?

What would you be thinking? We asked some of the players in our Academy that question and here were some of their answers:

"What are you thinking, coach?"

"You need to find somebody else."

"I can't miss this."

Can we agree that none of those responses listed would project confidence?

Here's what confidence would look like in that situation:

1. You have **trust in your ability to be courageous** (go all-in) in that moment regardless of what happens.

Do you see how you are tying your confidence to something internal that's within your control (Courage)? Your success is tied to your ability to detach from the result and "go all-in" in that moment. If your confidence was tied to the outcome in this situation—and you are 0–5 from the three-point line, how would that look? It would look like the three answers from above. See the difference?

What About Results?

It truly is a mind shift.

Player: I get it. But what happens when I go back to my practice and my coach (who doesn't think like this) is yelling at me for the mistakes that I make?

Me: Do you have full control over whether or not your coach yells at you?

Player: No.

Me: What do you have control over?

Player: How I handle my coach yelling at me.

Me: The question becomes: Do you have enough *self-trust* to listen to your inner coach (instead of your coach) in that situation?

Player: Yeah. But that will take a lot of confidence.

Nobody said it was easy. In fact, it's one of the hardest things that you will do. That's why so many people struggle with confidence.

Important: *Having a positive inner coach that you can trust is critical for confidence. The next five tools will match the tools used in the Positive section. We will look at how to build confidence using them.*

Dealing With Expectations

Blakely told me, "I feel so much pressure." I asked her, "Where is the pressure coming from?" She told me that it's coming from the expectations that she has for herself and the expectations that others place on her. Before we did anything, I asked her to write a letter to pressure (as if it were a person) and describe the impact that pressure has had on her life. I needed to better understand the relationship that she has with pressure.

Dear Pressure,

I cannot stand you. I cannot stand the overpowering feeling you give me at times. You engulf my entire body, my mind, and my thought process. You make me feel that there is no other option but success. You take away my joy, my pleasure, and my happiness. But thank you.

As much as I hate you, I love you. I adore you, in fact. I could not live, or play, without you. Without you I wouldn't be me, I wouldn't be the person that I am. I thrive off of you. Thank you for giving me your absolute worst, but making me my absolute best.

-Blakely

This letter showed me that she had a love/hate relationship with pressure. The good news: Blakely recognized the great things that pressure does for her. As I read the letter, it became apparent that she had become smothered by pressure. I asked her to do something for me.

Tool: Best Friend Advice

I asked Blakely to pretend that her best friend was in the exact same situation. I asked her to give her best friend advice on the best way to handle the situation. Blakely had some time to think about it. Here's what she wrote:

Set a time in your schedule (because I like schedules) after you complete your work, training, errands, etc. and take that time to escape from everything. Almost convert your mind into thinking that nothing else exists except for what you are doing in that moment. Whether that is reading a book, watching a movie, or eating cheesecake, commit to that and do not think or worry or "stress" about any other thing in your life during that time. You can work on this daily by having what you call your "Pressureless Time." And hopefully with that practice, you will get in the habit of knowing how to flip that switch when you want to, to continue to grow with it.

If you are giving advice to your best friend, it's based in love and care, and when you take that advice as your own, that's great dialogue with an inner coach. When your inner coach becomes somebody that gives you advice based on love and care, that's what a positive (good and useful) inner coach looks like. Here's where confidence comes into play.

Confidence equals self-trust. When you trust yourself, you trust your inner coach. You do that by taking your own advice. Confidence is essential for leadership because if you won't listen to your own advice, why would anybody else listen to you?

Confidence grows when you trust a good and useful inner coach.

Dealing With Failure

Here's a fact: you will experience failure on your path toward excellence. If failure is inevitable on your journey, the question then becomes: How do you manage failure so it doesn't affect your confidence? I was having a conversation with a player about this.

The player told me, "When I have success, I move to the next thing pretty quick. When I have failure, it takes me until the next game to move on."

I asked him, "If the game is two days away, does it take you two days to get over it?"

Player: It's a rough two days.

Me: Can we agree this is a fact? You are going to get over the failure.

Player: Yes.

Me: Why not get a head start? Instead of being disappointed for two days, why not get a two-day head start?

Player: When you break it down like that, I need to.

Those two days of disappointment can create a lot of self-doubt. Which is the enemy of self-trust. How can you build self-trust in a moment of failure? By planning for it.

Tool: Plan Positive

This player knows that there will be times when he experiences failure. He can plan the content and tone of that situation so the next time he's in that situation he can build self-trust by listening to a good and useful inner coach. If we filled out a Plan Positive card it would look like this:

Tough Situation: lost a game.

Content: "Get a head start." Or, "Great opportunity to bounce back." (This will remind you to not waste energy beating yourself up. Instead, you can reinvest the energy into the next thing.)

Tone: Encouraging.

The next time that moment presents itself, you can build confidence by trusting your inner coach. You are placing your trust in your ability to be resilient (bounce back from setbacks).

When do we feel confident? We feel confident when we are in control. It is in our control to **trust our ability** to be resilient. If we plan our performance on how we handle the loss, then we just have to trust ourselves to execute.

The player then asked me, "What if the people around you don't want you to get a head start? What if they hold you in the past by constantly talking about it?"

Me: What advice would you give to me in that situation?

Player: It doesn't matter how they view it. Try and explain the concept of getting a head start to the next thing and how it helps you. If they listen to you, that's great. If they don't, that shouldn't impact you. It then becomes an opportunity to build confidence. If the people around you are telling you something that you know doesn't work for you, it's a chance for you to trust yourself.

When this player said this to me, I knew that he got it. He converted a negative situation (where the people around him were holding him in the past) into an opportunity to grow.

Tool: Replace Negative

If your inner coach is saying to you, "You suck" and you trust your inner coach, how are you feeling about yourself? Not very good, right? A huge part of self-trust is listening to your inner coach. That's why it's critical for your inner coach to have "good and useful" thinking.

It's human nature to doubt yourself when you are struggling. One player told me, "My inner coach is quiet when things are good. It usually waits to show up and tell me when things are going bad." My experience is that a lot of players can relate to that statement. You know what the irony is? The tough moments are when you need your inner coach the most.

Think about this, when's the last time you doubted yourself? My guess is probably pretty recently. Clearly that's not good and useful thinking. So how do we get back to being confident? The goal should be to turn our inner coach into somebody who can guide us through the tough times by sending us messages that ensure our self-trust. We do this by replacing negative thoughts with positive thoughts, and then trusting them.

Here are the three steps to getting back to positive once you go negative using this example:

1. Acknowledge the thought:
   Example of a negative thought: *I can't do this.*
2. Interrupt the thought.
3. Replace the thought:
   Example of a positive thought: *You got this. Try it again.*

Replace thoughts that contain self-doubt with thoughts that contain self-trust.

Important: There is a difference between self-doubt and useful feed-back. The best athletes have a good inner coach but that doesn't mean that their inner coach can't point out things that they could do better (in a positive way) in order to improve.

I Hate Being Compared

Have you ever played on a team where your teammate got a lot of attention? There are a lot of challenges that come along with that situation. This hits home for a player who has a teammate that he's been compared to since he was in 8th grade. Both have plans to go to the same college.

They are both very good. However, this player's teammate was elected to the All-American team and he wasn't. It is a tough situation for this player, but not for the reason that we all might think. I was talking with him about it:

Me: How are you?

Player: It's tough.

Me: What's tough?

Player: Do I want to be an All-American? Of course. But I'm over that. You know what the hardest thing is? It's dealing with all of the questions. Are you OK? Are you upset your team-mate got it and you didn't? It's like, I'm over it, but everybody around me keeps bringing it up.

We looked at how we could turn this into an opportunity.

Tool: Opportunity Converter

We then talked about how we could convert this into an opportunity. We decided that this would allow him to under-stand how to help a future teammate who might go through the same thing. This experience will allow him to connect and relate to that future teammate on a much deeper level.

Do you see how we converted a situation that could lead to self-doubt (by not being validated) into an opportunity? This becomes a situation where he can learn how to continue to have self-trust even when he isn't being validated by external sources (what a great skill to have for life). We had a great conversation about it:

Me: A lot of people need validation to feel good about what they do. What do you think about that?

Player: I've always needed that.

Me: I think becoming dependent on validation from outside sources gets in the way of self-trust.

Player: How so?

Me: Think about sports: scoreboards, fans, and media are all forms of validation. They appear to tell us whether or not we do well. When you get into relationships, all that goes away. Nobody is there to be like, "Man, way to show patience in that conversation." You have to learn to listen to yourself and trust yourself.

Player: That's pretty awesome. I would have never thought about it like that.

That was one of my favorite conversations that I had with him. If this player hadn't gone through that situation, we would have never had the opportunity to discuss how external validation gets in the way of self-trust. My hope is that he realizes that whether or not he is validated by the outside, that shouldn't affect the way he feels about himself.

Tool: Don Meyer Notebook

Use this as a tool. The next time you are in a situation where you are having a tough time moving on, get with a coach (or do it individually) and answer these two questions:

What did I do well and why?

What can I do better and how?

After performances, we have a tendency to remember and focus on all of the bad things that we did. This exercise helps you neutralize all of the emotions that you are feeling. When you answer these two questions it gives you a plan and a place to direct all of your energy. You go inside of yourself to find answers. Once you have your answers, self-trust is built by taking your own advice.

Confidence (self-trust) is all about the moment, isn't it? Do we have trust in our ability to handle the moment? Each moment gives us a unique opportunity to rely on ourselves.

When we attach our self-trust to something that's within our control (character skills) we build our confidence and it's a confidence that can be universally applied to all moments.

5 Ways to Exercise Confidence:

1. **Best Friend Advice:**
    If you are giving advice to your best friend, it's based in love and care. When you take that advice as your own, that's what good dialogue looks like from an inner coach. Confidence is built by trusting that advice.

2. **Plan Positive:**
    Plan the content and tone of your inner coach. Trust your inner coach and don't doubt yourself the next time you are going through failure and questioning your abilities.

3. **Replace Negative:**
    Pay attention to the dialogue in your head. When you see a thought that contains self-doubt ("I can't do this"), interrupt it and replace it with a thought that contains self-trust.

4. **Opportunity Converter:**
    Find situations where you doubt yourself. Convert that situation into an opportunity to build confidence.

5. **Don Meyer Notebook:**

Take the failure (and the achievement) and learn from it. By acquiring what the experience can teach you, it will lead to a deeper level of self-trust.

☑ Courageous

I asked Kenny, "What does your coach do when you make a mistake?"

He said, "He subs me out."

Me: How does that affect you?

Kenny: I'm afraid to make mistakes.

Me: Is it difficult to "play free" in these conditions?

Kenny: I feel pressure to play perfect because I don't want to come out.

Me: It takes courage to overcome that. Let's learn how to put fear in second place.

Courage > Result

Put yourself in this situation: you're a senior, the team's best player, and the captain. In the last two games, you've come up big by hitting the game-winning shots.

Last night was one of those nights.

As you sit in the film room (the day after hitting the second game winner) you think about how close you are to winning the conference championship. Then your coach walks into the film room to address the team before practice starts. Your head coach immediately singles you out. He starts to show the team film of you.

But instead of showing the clips of you hitting the game-winning shots, he surprises you. He's taken clips of you from the past three years. All of the clips have one thing in common: they're of you coming up short in clutch situations. In other words, they're clips of you in the exact same situation that you were in the past two games—but they show you missing those shots.

After the collage of (what society would deem unsuccessful) clips your coach addresses you. He says, "You know why you were successful the past two games? Despite all of these situations where you've come up short, you continue to put yourself in the situation because you aren't afraid of the moment. Winners fail. Losers hide."

"Winners fail. Losers hide." When a coach says that, what signal does that send to the team? I asked the players in our Academy and they said, "The coach cares more about the player having the courage to take the shot versus whether or not the shot goes in."

This coach has redefined failure. He's taken the emphasis away from the result. Failure to this coach is not going for it, which is a high-level mentality. Is it any wonder why his players would value courage? Compare that to the following situation I went through when I was a player.

S-T-U-P-I-D

We were playing a top team in the country and the coach draws up the last play of the game for me. I run the play, I take the shot, and I miss the shot. We lose.

After missing the game-winning shot, I head into the locker room and sit down. The head coach singles me out in front of the team. He asks me a question that I don't answer the way he wants me to answer.

He takes a dry-erase marker and comes up and writes S-T-U-P-I-D across my forehead in front of everybody in the room. You could hear a pin drop in the locker room.

How would you feel if a coach wrote S-T-U-P-I-D on your forehead after you missed a game-winner? We asked the players in our Academy. They responded: humiliated, useless, hurt, defeated, and discouraged.

What makes the coach that I played for different from the first coach that I mentioned in the previous example? The coach from the first example is coaching a different game. We've all played for coaches similar to the one in the second situation (hopefully not quite as dramatic). They make it tough for players to have courage.

What did the coach in the first situation do so well? He made it clear to the team that courage has nothing to do with the outcome. It has everything to do with going all-in and being OK with falling on your face. **Winners fail. Losers hide.**

Surround yourself with an inner circle that is supportive: a group of people who value you going for it (when it's outside your comfort zone) versus whether or not it works out. That's critical.

Here's our definition for Courage:

Courage: Operating outside your comfort zone.

High Dive

You have two options when it comes to a challenge:

1. You can hide from it.
2. You can chase it.

Where does personal growth happen? It happens when you approach challenges. Kevin Love, an NBA player, told me that his philosophy in life is: "Life begins at the edge of your comfort zone." High achievers learn to live there.

JoAnne McCallie, women's basketball coach at Duke University, did an exercise to illustrate to her team what it looks like to approach fear. She had a few girls on her team that had never learned how to swim. Guess what they did? JoAnne explains:

I had our team jump off the high dive. I had each team member jump off and of course there were various levels of abilities to swim. The idea was: the team was around the deep end and would help the teammate as they struggled.

(We did have a lifeguard on duty—just so you know.)

JoAnne told me that one of her girls took over 45 minutes to jump.

Disclaimer: I do not recommend doing this with your team for obvious liability reasons.

Is it an extreme example? Yes. But here's what I take away: it's a wonderful illustration of what courage looks like. It's literally a leap of faith to "go all-in." It also highlights that when we have a circle of support, it makes it easier for us to leave our comfort zone and go for it.

Option 1 or Option 2

What prevents people from getting out of their comfort zone? Fear. The fear is tied to the outcome and all of the things that come with the outcome.

I was talking with a player named Tyler about this. He told me that he was playing tentatively. We started to explore why:

Me: Why are you playing tentatively?

Tyler: Every time I make a mistake my coach takes me out.

Me: So you play tentatively so you don't make mistakes?

Tyler: Yes.

I gave Tyler two options to choose from:

Option 1: Go all-in. Risk being taken out of the game for the chance to be great.

Option 2: Eliminate the chance of being great by playing tentatively and not getting taken out of the game.

He said, "When you put it like that—option 1. I never thought about it like that."

Can you relate to that? Tyler was blinded by fear. In his case, he was afraid of being taken out of the game. The fear was getting in the way of him being great. In order for us to be all that we can be we have to learn how to put fear in second place. I showed Tyler something that we did with a soccer team.

Playing Free

I was working with the University of Florida's soccer team and their head coach, Becky Burleigh. One of the things we emphasized leading up to the Elite 8 was that we really wanted the players to play free. Playing free means not tightening up, which is really tough for players when there's a lot on the line. We've found that when there's more on the line, that feeling of anxiety gets even more intense.

One of the things that makes post-season soccer interesting is it's played outdoors. Weather conditions aren't predictable. The University of Wisconsin played a post-season game with two-and-a-half inches of snow on the ground.

We showed pictures of that game to the team to help them understand that we have to be ready for anything. Obviously these aren't ideal weather conditions for a sport that requires you to pass the ball on the ground.

We then showed the team a picture taken at Winthrop University with puddles all over the field. Again, not the best conditions to pass a ball on the ground. After showing the team the picture at Winthrop, we put a picture of one of Florida's former players on the screen:

Shana is the player pictured in this photo. We said to the team, "This is what it looks like to go all-in." We then asked them to think of a stoplight. We said, "This is what the color green looks like."

We then asked, "If this is what green looks like, what does yellow look like?"

The team described yellow as, "Playing cautious, taking less risks and playing timid."

The team made a goal: "play green" for each other.

Play Green

Before practice that day, we gave them Green Packages that contained 2 green wristbands. Everybody wore them as a visual reminder to each other to "play green." The goal: anybody who feels like they are going yellow, there are visual reminders everywhere to "play green."

The green wristbands gave everybody the reminder of the courage needed to chase the win, not avoid the loss. Was it effective? Fast forward to the Elite 8 game against Stanford.

Stanford was a number-one seed and they gave up two goals *the entire season* on their home field. They scored 34. That means the score on their field was 34-2. Within the first couple of minutes Stanford scores. You can imagine what most teams would feel in this moment.

We film the bench—it helps us coach everybody and it also allows us to see who is a great teammate. We caught the bench after the first goal. They were holding up their green wristbands to visually remind the team to reset and "go all-in." It was amazing.

We scored within 5 minutes.

They scored again.

We scored again.

Soccer is interesting because it's the only sport where you can tie and not move on. Stanford advanced in a penalty kick shootout. In the press conference after the game Becky said, "This was the most fulfilling year I've ever coached. It was amazing to see the players grow over the course of the year."

That team set the standard for what it means to "go all-in." We decided at the end of the year that we were going to embed this into the culture moving forward. Here are the designs of the jerseys for next year.

Notice the green dot on the shoulder. Now every time each player puts her jersey on, there is a visual reminder about what we are about. We "play green" for each other. I've presented this idea to a lot of teams across all sports and there seems to be a universal application. Players have told me that they draw a green circle (in the shape of a stoplight) on their wrist to help them reset.

One swimmer told me that she painted her toenails green as a visual reminder to "go all-in" right before she hit the water. The last thing swimmers see before they dive into the pool is their feet.

Back to Tyler

After I presented what I did with the University of Florida's soccer team to Tyler, I asked him, "What do you think about that?"

He said, "I like the idea."

Me: How could you use it?

Tyler: I can draw a green dot on my arm sleeve that I wear.

Me: How would you use it?

Tyler: If I start to play yellow I can look at the green dot to reset. It's a reminder for me to stay aggressive.

Tyler had a game a few days later. He missed two free throws late in the game. That's a tough spot to be in. He bounced back from those two free throws without getting down, and on the next offensive possession he delivered a game-winning play.

After the post-game press conference, Tyler's coach said, "I was proud. I could see Tyler's body language was good after the two free throws I watched him try to gather and regroup himself. I'm glad he did that. He kept us in the game."

I sent Tyler a text with the newspaper article in it. He sent me a text back saying, "The green dot really helped me!"

The Courage Zone

How can you train courage? Picture a small circle (like the one below) as your comfort zone.

Anything outside of your comfort zone is what we call the courage zone.

Anytime you get out of your comfort zone, what happens? Your comfort zone stretches.

Here's how I illustrate this to high-school guys. I'll tell them, "Think of the coolest, best-looking single person in your school. Everybody have it?"

Once I see a head nod from everybody, I then ask, "Would you be comfortable asking that person to the movies? Raise your hand if the answer is yes."

Once you have a hand raised—that's when things get interesting. In this case, Luke raised his hand. We had a conversation:

Me: Who is the girl?

Luke: Amber.

Me: Guess what's going to happen tomorrow?

Luke: What?

Me: You're going to ask Amber to go to the movies with you.

Luke: (Silence)

This is not an uncommon response. The room starts to heat up when you nudge people outside of their comfort zone and expose them to fear. They usually go silent. To make sure Luke showed courage and followed through, we had him fill out an accountability card for that week.

For him to get his card back, he'd have to ask Amber out. He did. She said yes.

Should I Text Her?

Confrontation is something a lot of players struggle with. I was talking with a player who didn't know how to approach a teammate who was disrupting team chemistry.

Player: I'm having a problem with a teammate.

Me: What's the matter?

Player: She gossips about people and it's becoming a team-wide issue.

Me: Have you confronted her about it?

Player: No.

Me: Why?

Player: I'm afraid of how she's going to react.

Me: Do you think you should?

Player: Yes. Should I text her?

We shared a laugh when I told her that I thought this was a face-to-face kind of thing. I've found that being honest (telling the truth) when confronting a difficult personal situation is one of the things that players struggle with the most. We started to work through how she was going to address her teammate.

Player: I don't even know where to start.

Me: Perfect. Start by telling her that.

Player: I don't want to hurt her feelings.

Me: Tell her that.

Player: (Laughing) I'm scared.

Me: Tell her that.

This player was coming from a good place—she just needed to articulate her thoughts. Confronting the truth takes courage. Here's how a coach puts her players in a position to practice confrontation.

Don't Cosign

When you cosign on something, you give your endorsement. Teri McKeever, a successful swim coach at University of California, Berkeley, uses a mantra with her team. She says, "Don't cosign on a teammate's behavior that hurts the team."

How do you cosign? According to her, there are two ways:

1. Agreeing with a teammate because you don't want to upset the person.
2. Not saying anything at all.

Let's return to the scenario from above and pretend you're in that situation. If you don't confront your teammate who is gossiping, what are you doing? You're cosigning on her behavior. Why do people co-sign? It usually comes down to one of two things:

1. People are afraid of the conflict.
2. People get stuck on what to say.

Teri does something with her team to help with this. She told me, "We do a team retreat. One of the things that we do on the retreat is set up role-playing scenarios. An example might be: your teammate is partying too much. What do you say to them? They then role-play it out. It helps them get ahead of the situation so they're more comfortable handling it when it happens."

It takes a lot of courage not to cosign. Here's an example of how I did the role-playing exercise with a player who struggles with her father.

Dealing With Dad

I was working with a player who had a difficult relationship with her dad. After she got done playing, her dad came over and yelled, "I can't believe that we spent all of this money on you and you go out there and play like that." (That's the edited version.) This tore her up. It was very uncomfortable for this player to talk about. We had a conversation about it:

Me: Why do you feel like you can't talk to anybody about your dad?

Player: It's like, I can be mad at my dad but nobody else can.

Me: You know what I love? Your loyalty. Can we try something? It's going to take a lot of courage?

Player: Yes.

Me: (I put an empty chair in front of her.) Can you pretend that your dad is sitting in this chair? Can you tell me what you wish you had the courage to tell him?

Player: I feel like I don't know where to start.

Me: That's perfect. Start there.

What happened for the next five minutes was amazing. It was emotional. But the strength that she had to discuss what she was going through was incredible. I wrote her words down as she spoke them:

I wish you could see how much I want to achieve all of my goals, how much I hate disappointing you, and how much time I put into what I want. You have made me scared of failing and it's held me back. I'm sorry you've put in the time and I don't live up to the standard. I know that you love me a lot.

It hurts me that you have a lot of issues that you need to deal with because you are hurting the family. It hurts me that you don't deal with them. You could be such a wonderful person if you could see areas that you can improve. I wish we had a relationship outside of my sport. I don't feel like I have a man in my life, and I wish that could be you.

That took a tremendous amount of courage. If this player wasn't able to do that I would have never been able to connect and process these issues with her.

5 Ways to Exercise Courage

1. **Redefine Failure:**
   Think about the coach's message to the senior who hit the two game-winners. He said, "Winners fail. Losers hide." What did this do for the player? It reframed failure. Failure became not going all-in and taking risks. Success became going after it and embracing whatever came with it.

   I heard a great coach once say, "There's winning and learning. There's no such thing as losing."

2. **Supportive Circle:**
   Think about the high-dive activity. The players that didn't know how to swim were put in a position (literally) to take a leap of faith. Where were their teammates? In the pool ready to provide support if needed. To me, that's what it looks like to have a supportive circle. Your circle provides support while you confront difficult situations.

   Reflect: Do you have anybody in your circle that undermines your courageousness? Do they make you feel the way my coach made me feel when he wrote S-T-U-P-I-D on my forehead? If so, how are you going to handle it? You might need to have a tough conversation with that person (or people).

3. **Put Fear in Second Place:**
   Courage is putting fear in second place by operating outside of your comfort zone. Make a list: What do you fear that's getting in the way of who you want to be? Maybe it's expressing emotions to people that are close to you? Maybe it's having a tough conversation with a teammate? Maybe it's approaching the girl that you wish you had the courage to?

   Whatever the fear, approach it. Find a way to leave your comfort zone once a day.

4. **Play Green:**
   Think of a stoplight. Define what yellow is to you. Then, commit to playing green. Draw a green circle that can serve as a reset button when you feel yourself start to go yellow in a game.

   Whether it's drawing a green circle on your wrist, your armband or (as the swimmer did) painting your toenails. Whatever you do, find a way to bring it into the game so you have a visual reminder to be aggressive.

5. **Don't Cosign:**
   You endorse behavior by:
   1. Agreeing with a teammate because you don't want to upset the person.
   2. Not saying anything at all.

   Confronting the truth isn't easy. Use the empty chair exercise to help you gather your thoughts. Pretend the person you want to speak to is in the chair and you have the courage to address him or her—what would you say? Use that as practice for the real conversation.

☑ Resilient

I asked Kenny, "Do you want to be more resilient?" (Bouncing back from setbacks.)

Kenny responded, "Yeah."

Me: Can we agree that the only way you can get better at bouncing back from setbacks is to have setbacks?

Kenny: Yeah.

Me: Then why would you fear them? Resilience is on the other side of that setback.

Kenny: (Laughing)

Me: Here's a story about some work I did with the softball team at the University of Florida.

Lunchboxes, Gum, and Bouncy Balls

I've had the privilege of working with Tim Walton. Tim coaches softball at the University of Florida. Each year he has a theme with his team. This year started with him handing out old-school lunchboxes. The theme: we come to work every-day. To build on this blue-collar mentality he gives every team member a time card.

Everybody clocks in when they come to the field. Everybody clocks out when they leave the field. It's a creative way to separate *who they are* from *what they do*.

I was at a game where #1 Florida was taking on #2 LSU at home. LSU got off to a good start and scored nine runs that game. Then Florida came back and scored ten runs.

After the game, one of Florida's players said, "We just scored 10 runs on the #2 team in the country. Bouncing back is a mindset."

When players echo the coach's message—that's a great thing. We used that quote to make resilience real. We found a picture of that player from the game and put the quote over her image.

We made 4x6 pictures and laminated them. Guess where we put them? That's right, in their lunchboxes. At the end of the season, members of the team will have a lunchbox full of memories that will illustrate how they grew together as people.

After that game, Tim also put a piece of gum in their lunch-box. He said, "The gum represents what it looks like to be resilient. No matter how much it's chewed on, it never goes away."

Pretty cool, huh?

I was telling a person (who plays volleyball at a very high-level) that story. She told me, "When you tell me that, you know what I think about?"

Me: What?

She said, "I think of a bouncy ball. If the ground is a setback, or if the wall is a setback—if you throw the ball at it, what does it do? It fires back. It doesn't just fall down. It redirects its energy."

I thought that was great analogy because how long does a bouncy ball stay on the wall or the ground once it hits it? One person in our Academy responded, ".0001 seconds." What if we could redirect our energy from a setback that quickly? That's this person's goal.

Guess what she's doing to help remind herself of her goal before each game? She's keeping a bouncy ball in her gym bag. Each time she takes her shoes out to get ready for a game— she'll see the bouncy ball as a reminder. It will remind her that whatever the game throws at her that day, she will bounce back from it…in *".0001 seconds."*

I told Tim (softball coach) this story and guess what he did? He put bouncy balls in everybody's lunchbox.

Dealing With Setbacks

In Part I a coach asked his player these three questions about a basketball game:

Coach: Would you be upset if you shoot less than 50%?

Player: Yes.

Coach: Would you be upset if you have 5 or more turnovers?

Player: Yes.

Coach: Would you be upset if you lose?

Player: Yes.

We looked at Kyrie Irving's first three years in the NBA. This is how often one or more of those things happened to him:

1st Year: 86%
2nd Year: 81%
3rd Year: 85%

We did the exact same research for Kevin Durant. Kevin will go down as one of the best scorers in the history of the NBA. We compared the first year of his NBA career to his MVP year and looked for how often one or more of those things happened to him:

Rookie Year: 95%
MVP: 67%

Think about that for a second. Even in Kevin Durant's MVP year, he was dealing with adversity the majority of the time.

(Most people don't know that Kevin Durant's record for his first two seasons in the NBA was 43 wins, 121 losses.)

What does this show us? Everybody deals with mistakes. It's important for younger players to understand that even the best players in the world deal with adversity a large majority of the time.

Why? Think about SportsCenter–what do you see? Highlights. When you watch SportsCenter you are seeing all of the great plays that players make. It creates an illusion that they don't deal with adversity as much as they do.

Recruiting

Here's a question for you: Why would a college coach want to watch a player (that they're recruiting) when they have an off game?

What does that expose? It exposes how they handle adversity. A lot of times when players lose or play poorly, it exposes things that winning hides. It gives you a better idea of how they handle adversity personally, and how it affects the way they interact with their teammates as they go through it.

Put yourself in this situation: a college coach comes to recruit you. In the game they come to watch you foul out in the first quarter of play.

What would you be thinking as you sat on the bench?

Would you view that as a:

Threat: "Man…there goes that scholarship."

Opportunity: "This is a great opportunity to show them how good of a teammate I can be from the bench."

If you are being honest, which are you picking? If you're like most athletes, you are processing it as a threat.

Here's the thing: that situation actually happened to a player. Buzz Williams was coaching basketball at Marquette University when it happened. He explained what he saw:

Buzz Williams, Basketball Coach, Virginia Tech University

The rest of the game, it was almost as if he was the coach on the team. He was an outstanding teammate, he was always positive. He was helping from the bench. He was helping during the timeouts. His body language was unbelievable.

The coach said after the game, "Buzz, I'm sorry he didn't play very well." I said, "I saw everything that I needed to see."

He played as bad as you could possibly play but everything that surrounded that game told me about the character of who he was. That was the only time I saw him play and he's ended up being our best player.

That player viewed his adversity (fouling out) as an opportunity to be a great teammate from the bench. High-achievers find ways to repurpose adversity into an opportunity to be better.

Stephen Curry

Stephen Curry, an NBA player, is another great example of someone who demonstrated that he could handle adversity during the recruiting process. The game hasn't come easy for Stephen Curry. But he's become one of the best players in the world despite being somewhat undersized. Bob McKillop, who coaches at Davidson University, talked about a time he saw Stephen play during the recruiting process and how it had a lasting impression on him:

Bob McKillop, Basketball Coach, Davidson University

When I recruited Stephen, he was in an AAU tournament in Las Vegas. I walked into the back gym of this facility and there he was going up and down the court. In the first half, I believe he had 9 turnovers. And yet as he had a turnover he'd still run back on defense.

He'd still clap his hands. He wouldn't blame an official. He wouldn't blame a teammate. He'd listen to the coach and he continued to play as hard as he could no matter the mistake he just made.

Think about how you would be in that situation. If you had nine turnovers (that's a pretty horrific stat) how would you be? Would you do all of the things that he did? Do you see why it benefits coaches to see how you handle mistakes?

The story gets better. Stephen ends up going to Davidson to play for Bob. Bob explains his first game:

In his first game, playing against Eastern Michigan he had 9 turnovers in the first half—it was the exact same experience that I saw while I recruited him. I saw the way he handled it as a high school kid, I therefore believed in him at halftime. (We were down 18 points.)

I kept him in the game and we wound up winning.

The next night, he dropped 32 on the University of Michigan in his second college game. And it's the great lesson that he's never going to get down about adversity. He's going to use adversity as opportunity. He's going to continue to stay focused on what he can control and it's clear that he's done that as a member of Golden State and of course in the great success that he had at Davidson College.

Nobody wants to make mistakes. Basketball (like all sports) is a game of mistakes. What if you started to work on how you handle the mistake, instead of the mistake itself? The game provides a lot of opportunity to do so.

List Out Opportunities For Resilience

The transition from playing your sport in high school to college is challenging for many reasons.

Here's an example: in high school, a player won the Player of the Year Award. When she got to college nearly everybody on the team had won that award. And all of them were older and had more experience.

I was talking with this player and I asked her, "How's it going?"

She told me, "I love it here when I play good. But I hate it here when I play bad."

I asked her to explain.

She said, "I hate being bad at something and here's the thing, I realize that I have to grow my game. I understand that means that there are going to be things that I'm bad at before I get good at them. I don't handle that well."

Resilience is the answer to handling it better. After we talked about how important that is, I asked her, "Do you want to be more resilient?"

She said, "Yes."

Then I asked, "Well, how can we use your sport to help you with that?"

We then made a list of all the opportunities that her sport provides to help her build resilience. Here were some of the examples:

- Turnover
- Bad call
- Mental error
- Getting yelled at
- Being subbed out
- Injury

We then repositioned how we see these things. To most people, it may appear that when these things happen, they are failing. We repurposed these situations into opportunities to grow resilience. (Opportunity Converter.)

I did this exercise with a high-level volleyball team. The team listed out some of the setbacks that their game offers them:

- Shanking a pass or dig
- Hitting error
- Missed serve
- Getting blocked
- Injury
- Making the wrong read

After we listed out (as a group) the setbacks that we'd be dealing with, we talked about the "Next Play Mentality."

Next Play Mentality

I ask players: Do you struggle with moving past making mistakes? A lot of players have a tough time with this. Mike Krzyzewski was the first coach to introduce me to a concept called "Next Play Mentality."

He said, "You cannot do anything for the last play. In other words, someone who is always looking in his rearview mirror will never make the most of the current moment. So the next play is the next moment. Why wouldn't you want to be at your best for the next moment?"

That's strong logic.

We tell players that regardless of what just happened (good or bad) don't focus on the past because you can't control that.

What can you control?

You can move on and be at your best for the next play.

I asked Mike, "When you see a player not react negatively to a mistake, what does that show you?"

He said, "When a player doesn't show a reaction after making a mistake, he's reached a level of maturity that you need to reach to be a really good player. The game is a game of mistakes. You are going to make mistakes in this game. It's too fast. Nobody is perfect. You can't let one mistake lead to another mistake."

Basketball (like many other sports) is a game of mistakes–how you handle those mistakes is critical for your performance.

3751

Have you ever had a player on your team who brought unbelievable positive energy when they were playing well? And when they played poorly, they did the exact opposite? That can be destructive to a team.

Here's one way a coach illustrated the "Next Play Mentality" to a player.

Here was the player's stat line: he played 38 minutes and made 2 shots out of 11. The coach asked him three questions the next day:

Coach: How many minutes did you play last night?

Player: 38 minutes.

Coach: How many shots did you miss?

Player: 9 shots.

Coach: How long does it take you to shoot a shot once you get the ball?

Player: (A little confused) About a second.

Coach: Let me get this straight. You allowed 9 seconds (9 shots/1 second per shot) to affect the rest of the 37 minutes and 51 seconds that you played?

Think about that for a second. Don't let the minority (in this case 9 seconds) affect the majority (37:51).

Coming Up Short

Blakely's team was favored to win their conference tournament. In the first round of tournament, the game went to shootout penalty kicks.

Blakely missed hers and her team went on to lose.

A few days later...

I had a conversation with Blakely. I asked, "What were you thinking about as you kicked it?"

She told me, "Honestly, I couldn't get the penalty kick that I missed with the national team out of my head."

Earlier in the year, Blakely was in a similar situation with the national team and she missed. That's how the national team's journey ended.

Rearview Mirror versus Windshield

Here's what I did: I took Blakely out to the practice field. There was a ball on the PK line and her assistant coach stood there. They spoke for a few minutes about the technical aspects of her form.

After that, I brought out a chair to the line and asked Blakely to sit down. I handed her a mirror. Her coach had a few sheets of paper and stood behind her. We asked Blakely to look in the mirror and read the papers that her coach was holding up.

What Blakely was reading were past headlines of articles that were written about her. Here's what they said:

North Korea Advance On Blakely's Weak Effort From The Spot

Blakely Denied On PK At Conference Tourney

Blakely Choices Affecting Her Play

After she read the headlines from her past. We created new (future) headlines that she read. Her coach then stood in front of her and Blakely read them out:

Blakely Bounces Back, Hits PK

Person > Player Proves Successful

Blakely Leaves Great Legacy At University

What point were we trying to illustrate? What's in her rear-view mirror? The past. It's hard to be at our best when our focus is there. What we needed to focus on was the windshield.

What's in her windshield? The present moment that's leading her to a bright future.

Blakely asked to hang the headlines in her room. She had two goals the next game in the opening round of the NCAA tournament.

Exercising Resilience

Can you practice being resilient? Here's one way a basketball team did.

Their mantra for the year was: "Be Road Tough."

Here's what they did to create a space in practice to where they could actually exercise resilience.

When the team scrimmaged the assistant coaches were the refs.

Think about this: Do you get better calls from refs at home or on the road? Most people will answer at home, right?

When the team scrimmaged, the refs (assistant coaches) would give them "road calls." The players would have to learn how to play through bad calls.

If there was a negative reaction or they didn't move on to the next play quickly–they would have to come out and sit for a minute.

The way it was positioned:

If you're reacting negatively, you aren't in the game mentally. Why should you be in the game physically?

When a player sits out for not being resilient, they aren't being penalized. What's happening? The coaches are rewarding the team that is being resilient by giving them an advantage. Do you see how it's framed in a positive way?

The goal: encourage the players to "Be Road Tough."

Develop a Failure Recovery System

Sue Enquist is the former coach of the UCLA softball program. She was a part of 11 national championships. She talks about how her "Failure Recovery System (FRS)" was one of the key pieces to her success. It was non-negotiable.

What does that mean? How would society define failure? Not reaching your goal. So, is your goal to drop a ball? Obviously not, so that would be considered a failure. Let's say that happens in a softball game. Here's how Sue would coach her team through failure—it's a planned performance.

If a player commits an error they have three steps they have to take:

1st Step: They pat their chest twice. (That means, "I own the failure. I **am not** a failure.")

2nd Step: Point to a teammate. (Let them know you've moved past the mistake.)

3rd Step: Call out the number of outs in that inning. (Let them know you are present.)

Here's what's interesting: let's say you're playing in a game and you make a mistake. What happens if you don't execute the "Failure Recovery System?" It's simple, you come out of the game.

Practicing Failing

Sue actually practices failure recovery with her team. Here's one way: they field groundballs. When they do, they have the first baseman sit on a bucket. This limits the mobility of the first baseman. Which means what? It increases the failure rate.

Then, every time there's a mistake, the coaches are zoomed in to see if the players execute the "Failure Recovery System."

Sue believes negative energy is poison to a team. If a player has negative energy after making a mistake, they watch the rest of practice away from the team in the stands. Pretty intense, right?

She says, "They learn pretty quickly that it's important."

Do you see how Sue practiced failing at UCLA? How could you practice failing?

5 Ways to Exercise Resilience:

1. **List Out Opportunities For Resilience:**
   Without setbacks, you can't build resilience. Create a list of setbacks that your sport offers you to build resilience. Repurpose all of those "setbacks" into an opportunity to get better and become a stronger person.

2. **Develop a Failure Recovery System:**
   Plan your performance before it happens. How do you want to handle your mistakes? What do you want to do? If you're a baseball player, what's your routine after a strikeout? If you're a basketball player, after a missed shot, how quickly can you get to the next play? If you're a golfer, how can you flush a bad shot and reset? If you have a planned routine to handle your setbacks, it helps you get to the next play faster.

3. **Practice Failing:**
   Practice your failure recovery. Spend 3 minutes pretending you just struck-out. Pretend you just missed a shot in basketball and work on getting back on defense with no reaction. As a golfer, practice flushing a bad shot. When you actually work on execution, it creates an awareness that can become a habit and carry over

into a game situation.

4. **Choose Challenge:**
Put yourself in a position that will challenge you, that way you will get more experience dealing with setbacks. Here are a few examples:

- Pick Teammates that Aren't as Good:
When you scrimmage (or play pick-up) play with people that will challenge you the most. In team sports, pick teams in a way that you are at a clear disadvantage.

- Don't Call Fouls:
Make a rule: never call a foul. See if you can get to a point where the contact and disadvantage doesn't affect you.

- Create a Disadvantage:
Sue Enquist had her first baseman sit on a bucket to limit her mobility. Soccer coaches shrink the space (make the field smaller) and use smaller goals, so it's harder to score. Lacrosse uses what are called "fiddle stix"—they have a smaller pocket that makes it harder to receive the ball.

How could you create a physical disadvantage?

- Create Come-from-behind Situations:
Create a game within a game. When you play someone who's not as good as you one-on-one—for you to win, you have to score 11 points but you have to hold them to under 5 points. By doing that, you've created a situation mentally where you're down 6–0 to start the game.

5. **Watch Film of Mistakes:**
   Most sports are games of mistakes. Find ways to clip your mistakes from practice or games and grade how you respond to each mistake. As you watch yourself right after the mistake, ask yourself: Is that who I want to be? What story am I telling people that are there to watch and support me?

Important: *The only way you can build resilience is to have setbacks —embrace adversity...it will make you stronger.*

☑ Competitive

After we got done talking about resilience, Kenny asked me, "How do I get better at not comparing myself to others?"

I asked Kenny, "Do you believe competition is a comparison?"

He said, "I never thought about it like that before. I guess it is."

Me: In your letter to basketball you wrote, *I want to be the best*. Let me ask you this: What's the difference between wanting to be the best versus wanting to be your best?

Kenny: You're not comparing yourself to others.

Me: Do you think if you viewed it that way it would help your relationships?

Kenny: No doubt.

Me: I believe when you look at competition as a rivalry—it's impossible to be your best self. I'm going to show you a healthy way to view competition. I think this will have a big impact on you.

The Drive to Win

If I asked you to define the word competitive, how would you do it? For example, if I said, "Man, that player is competitive," what would that mean to you? I love asking players that question.

After giving them 30 seconds to come up with their answers—I ask them this:

How many of you had the word "win" in your definition? (Nearly everybody raises his or her hand.)

Consider this conversation that I had with a player:

The player told me, "I've always known that I'm extremely competitive. Everybody has always told me that since I was young."

I asked, "What does the word competitive mean to you?"

He said, "Having the intensity or will to be better than the people that you are up against—having the will to win."

When you look at being competitive through that lens—*wanting to be better than*—I believe that leads to a deep negative internal conflict that makes it hard for good relationships with yourself and your teammates to flourish.

My Internal Conflict

I had a deep internal conflict when I was a freshman in college. It was the first time that I had lived away from home. I was rooming with my teammate.

Here's what made it a tough situation:
The teammate I roomed with played the same position as me.

What made it worse?
I liked him. He was a close friend and I wanted him to do well but (in my eyes) the only way he did well was at my expense.

What made it worse?
The coach would pit us against one another. It sounded like, "Brett, Mike's going to take your spot."

Think about that for a second. I had to sleep in the same room as this person. That can fracture a friendship, which can tear at a team.

The way I viewed it: I was in a win/lose situation. The only way I won was if he lost. And the only way he won was if I lost. This made it really hard for me to want to see him do well. It makes it very difficult to have a good friendship if you don't want the other person to do well.

Can you relate to that?

I can't tell you how many athletes shake their head and tell me, "Man, I've been in that situation."

Run Your Race

Mike Krzyzewski teaches all of his incoming freshmen a lesson. I can't tell you how helpful this story would have been for me when I was in that situation with my roommate. Here's the story he tells them:

Mike Krzyzewski, Basketball Coach,
Duke University

We tell every player that comes into our program: "Each of you run your own individual race and then collectively we're running a team race." I'll give you an example. Elton Brand and Shane Battier came in the same year.

Shane Battier was the National Player of the Year, Elton Brand was ranked—he was a McDonald's All-American, he was ranked about 18-20. Elton Brand was more ready to play though than Shane, you know, as far as his future. And so Elton Brand by the end of his sophomore year was the National Player of the Year, and the number one draft pick in the NBA.

If Shane Battier was running Elton Brand's race he'd be disappointed saying, "What's happening to me?" You know, Shane had a different race to run. Two years later, he was the National Player of the Year, he was the sixth pick in the NBA Draft.

I'm not saying everybody will be National Player of the Year, or be in the NBA Draft, I'm just saying that kids mature and come along some faster and then stop, some slower and then faster and some who never stop. You know, don't gauge yourself with what another kid is doing, gauge yourself on how you are doing.

That would have been a game-changer for me.

Competere

What if we redefined the way we look at what it means to compete? What if there was a healthier way to view competition? A way that would accent all of the positives that it can g? I think we would digest the forces of competition in a much different way.

Let's start here: Where does the word "compete" come from? It comes from the Latin root word *competere*, which means:

Competere: To strive together.

What if we viewed competing as striving together? What if we actually viewed competition as a partnership? Here's why we need competition.

Answer this question: When would you run faster?

1. By yourself
2. With someone else

What do you think the overwhelming majority of players tell me? The second answer: **with someone else**. Why? They have someone who is challenging them. What does this show? It shows us that our performance increases when others challenge us. In other words, we need other people to push us to a level that we couldn't get to on our own.

To us, we define compete as: to strive together.

Me <u>With</u> You

When you look at competition as a partnership things change.

Instead of: Me vs. You

We can replace the middle word and change it to:

Me **with** You

Then my contest is against myself from yesterday and your contest is against yourself from yesterday. We're there to make each other better. I need you to bring your best and I'll bring my best. But it's so we both benefit. Does that make sense?

What if we viewed competition this way? How would that help the internal relationships on your team? You've changed the opponent. You no longer look at your teammates as the enemy. They are your partners and you are striving together to make one another better.

The Power Four

Here are the four words centered around competing that you commonly hear used:

Compete: To strive together.

Competitor: A partner in challenge.

Competition: A partnership to challenge.

Competitive: To strive to be <u>your</u> best.

Unhealthy Competition (What it Looks Like)

I was working with a coach who had a dysfunctional culture among his players. The players would put each other down in hopes of trying to get their teammates to play bad so they could take their spot. When I met with the coaches, they showed me a list of their four core values. One of their values was: *compete.*

Underneath the word it was defined as: *strive to win something by defeating or establishing superiority over others who are trying to do the same thing.*

If this is how the team views competition, why wouldn't the players have dysfunctional relationships with each other? They are trying *to defeat and establish superiority* over each other. How can a good relationship (based on care) flourish in an environment where people don't want to see each other do well?

Think about it: How can you have a good relationship with somebody when you aren't pulling for that person?

That's like saying to your friend (who you care about), "Hope you don't get the spot."

How can a friendship exist when both people don't want to see the other do well? I don't think it can. But I do understand how it gets to this point.

They're Going to Take Your Spot

Let's say your coach says this to you, "If you don't play better (insert your teammate's name) is going to take your spot."

What has your coach just done? He's created a competition. Who's the opponent? Your teammate.

Do you want to see your "opponents" do well?

No.

So what's happening? You're actually rooting against your teammate.

When I tell this next point to players—they start laughing. They know it's true.

I ask, "If your teammate has the spot you want, it's not like you want to see them do terribly, you just want to see them do *bad enough* that you get their spot, right?" They start laughing and agree.

Who loses in this situation? The team.

That's My Story

I was telling Bryan, a former high-level tennis player, this story and he started laughing. He said, "That's my story."

Bryan told me that he was in a situation where he and another teammate were competing for the same spot, and it caused him a lot of internal conflict.

He took his teammate out to dinner and came clean. He told his teammate, "I root against you every day in practice."

His teammate laughed and said, "I do the same thing with you."

In that moment, they realized that there had to be a different way—a way that wouldn't tear at their friendship or the team chemistry.

What Healthy Competition Looks Like

Bryan learned a valuable lesson as a player. He is now a coach (who's won a national championship) at the highest level. If you go to a practice of his, you will see something completely abnormal. It's the definition of what it looks like to compete (strive together).

Bryan challenges his tennis players to lift the player across the net up by giving them encouragement. The goal: to help your teammate be his or her best so they challenge you more, so you'll be pushed to be at your best. That's what it looks like to strive together.

Here are three other great examples of how coaches facilitate healthy competition.

Example #1: In the Locker Room

I walked around the facility of a championship softball program. As I walked into the locker room, I noticed a decal on *every* mirror. The decal read: *Look in the mirror. That's your competition.*

I was amazed. As I went to exit the locker room, I noticed a sign hanging on the door. It said *Win The Moment.*

Every player I came across in this program wore a green rubber band that said *Competere (Strive Together).*

Example #2: On the Schedule

The first day of practice, a baseball coach walked into the locker room and said, "I have our schedule for the year."

He started to hand the schedules out to his players and as the players received the schedules they looked at them and smiled. All of the schedules read:

Date:	Opponent:	Time:
Feb. 13	Us	7:00 p.m.
Feb. 14	Us	7:00 p.m.
Feb. 15	Us	7:00 p.m.

What message was the coach trying to send to his team by giving them this schedule? They are competing with themselves within the game of baseball. Each game presents its own set of challenges that all offer an opportunity to make the team better.

Example #3: Post-Season

I was working with a team and we got together an hour before the NCAA tournament brackets were being released. We were having dinner.

The coach stood up and said to the team, "I already know who we play in the first round."

The team was surprised; they didn't think that information was released yet. They asked, "Who?"

The coach said, "Ourselves."

Everybody smiled. The team's message for the year was: #StriveTogether. They wanted to be the best version of themselves.

Note: All three of these coaches have won national championships at the highest level.

Kevin Durant – A True Competitor

Kevin Durant provides an excellent example of what striving together looks like. Here's something that Kevin told me he started doing as a freshman when he played basketball at the University of Texas:

Kevin Durant, NBA Player

One thing I try not to do is be a guy that goes into the gym and wants to be the only guy in the gym. I don't want to be the guy that says "I was working today, what were you doing?" I want to pull my teammates into the gym with me. If I work hard and we all work hard, I know only good things can come out of it.

Why is that so impressive? Think about the earlier example: Are you going to pull your teammate into the gym with you if your coach pits you against one another? Chances are, you aren't because you want to stretch the gap between you and your teammate so you get the playing time.

That's why it makes what Kevin did so special. He's operating on a different level.

When Kevin goes into the gym by himself, does he get better? Yes. Do his teammates? No.

Now, if Kevin brings his teammates to the gym, does that affect his development at all? No, he still gets better. But who else gets better? His teammates. Which means the whole team gets better.

Important: Think back to the race example—when would you run faster, by yourself or with someone else? We push ourselves harder when others challenge us. In this example with Kevin, he might get even better with his teammates there because he has people pushing him.

Here's my question to you: Do you see the negative impact a coach can have on a team when he pits players against one another in practice? If you have a team full of competitors who are there to strive to bring out the best in themselves and others, then that's a perfect environment for team improvement.

What if you repositioned the way you view your teammates (even if your coach does pit you against them)? Instead of viewing your teammate as the enemy, view your teammate as a growth partner.

Question: If your teammate gets better, will you be more challenged?

Yes.

Do you see why it helps you to challenge your teammate to be their absolute best? It makes you better (and your relationship better).

Why Would I Do That?

Player rankings give you status. Status and recognition can get in the way of your development. When players get status at an early age, you know what starts to happen? They start to protect their status instead of seeking out challenges to discover more about themselves and their weaknesses.

Michael (who's a top-5 player in the country) and I were having a conversation about viewing competition in a different way. He asked me: "I understand viewing competition that way for your teammates, but why would you want the teams you play against to do well?"

I asked Michael a simple question: "Do you want to be an NBA MVP one day?"

Michael: Yes.

Me: Which will help you get there: Other teams at their best? Or at their worst?

Michael: Best.

Me: If that were the case, why wouldn't you want them to bring their best? It will raise your level.

When you view it this way *you no longer fear anybody*. You embrace the challenge of taking someone's best shot because you are interested in discovering more about yourself. The more you are challenged, the more you grow. A true competitor understands that.

Competition – A Partnership?

Another tennis coach told me that he had the two best players in the country on his team. They would go at each other to get the number one spot. It was a status thing. They competed like crazy for that spot to the point where it tore at the team.

You know what he did? He repositioned the competition between them.

He brought them in and sat them down. They could see the upcoming year's schedule on his desk. He picked the schedule up and handed it to them. He then told them, "Take a look at the schedule."

As the players picked up the paper, they saw red markings next to every match.

The coach had already marked who would be #1 for the entire year. He said, "You guys are going to share that spot. Each match you will alternate."

He then ended the meeting with, "You have one focus this year. I want you two to challenge each other in practice every day to make each other better."

Guess what happened? They won a national championship.

I told another coach this story and he told me, "Man, I am constantly putting guys up against one another and you know what happens? They start rooting against one another."

He realized that he was fueling the fire and that *he was a major contributor* to the reason his players weren't pulling for one another.

Change the opponent by redefining what competition is. Competition: a **partnership** to challenge each other. The goal for these two players became to bring their best each day in order to make the other person better. How cool is that? Their relationship improved. It gave them permission to bring their best so they could help the other person by challenging them with all they could handle.

Rivalry-Based Competition

A lot of the players that I meet with struggle with how they handle being compared to others. Is it any wonder why that happens? If your coach (or parent) compares you to another player, why wouldn't you do the same? Comparisons to your teammates can destroy player-to-player relationships inside the team and undermine what healthy competition looks like.

I have been working with two high school players that are the best in the state. They've alternated Player of the Year for the past two years. They're coming up on the third year and everybody compares them to each other.

We had a chat about it.

I asked them, "Why is there a rivalry between you two?" One of them started in, "It's really hard for me—I was in class the other day and my teacher asked me if I was going to shut you down."

The other player laughed.

She said, "That exact same thing happened to me this past week. My teacher asked me if I was going to beat you."

Think about that for a second. Put yourself in that world— why wouldn't you compare yourself to others when everybody (including your teachers) is doing the same thing?

Thank You, Competition

My goal with these two players was to reposition the way that they viewed each other. I wanted to squash the negativity that comes with rivalry. Instead of each of them being fueled by negative energy (fear that the other was going to be better) I wanted to help them be fueled by positive energy. I had each of them write a thank-you note to the other.

Player #1:

I want to start off by saying that you're a great basketball player. You've pushed me to push myself ever since 8th grade. You have taught me that it is okay to be really good friends with someone who can also be your biggest competitor.

I've lost games because of you, but at the end of the day, that's what makes me push myself beyond what is possible. When I don't feel like working out or running extra sprints, I think to myself: I know you are. So I do it. Thank you for making me better.

Player #2:

Thank you for being such a fierce competitor. Until I met you, I never knew what it felt like to truly compete with someone. You have made me a better player by forcing me not to get complacent. And, on top of that, you're an awesome person.

I sincerely hope that we continue to grow closer in the future.

How cool is that? Do you see how they have repositioned the way they see each other? They are no longer rivals. They are fueling themselves with positive energy by viewing one another as growth partners.

Our Partners

When you walk into the soccer locker room at the University of Florida, the first thing you will see is a sign that reads:

Our Partners

Around the border of the room is the logo of every team that they will play that year.

When you look to the front of the locker room you see a sign that reads:

#Strive Together

We have repositioned the teams that we play from opponents to partners. After every game as a team we write a thank-you note to the other team. (We don't send it.) We keep it and we put it up next to their logo in the locker room.

What does the thank-you note capture? It captures what we learned from that team. Here's an example:

Thank you for helping us learn how to deal with lots of emotion and forcing us to keep our composure. You provided ample opportunities for us to practice moral skills, which helped us to understand what it looks like to stay classy.

Amidst the adversity you brought, you also united us to have each other's backs. You showed us the power of positivity and the encouragement that our bench can bring. Tactically you reminded us that shape and communication are key ingredients to our success and to always play to the whistle.

Finally, you showed us how and when to reset our play and each other.

With Love,
The Gators

We wrote the thank-you notes to capture what we learned from the other team. It allowed us to return to those notes when we play other teams (in the future) that have similar styles.

When we view competition as a rivalry it's impossible to be our best self. The appreciation of our competitors is how we find healthy competition.

5 Ways to Build Competitiveness

1. **Redefine Competition:**
   Start by changing the way you view these four words when you hear them:

   Compete: To strive together.
   Competition: A partnership to challenge.
   Competitor: A partner in challenge.
   Competitive: To strive to be your best.

2. **Change the Opponent:**
   Make yesterday your opponent. Try to win the day by being the best version of yourself while striving to improve. Create visual reminders to help you remember who you are competing against. Whether it's a sign on your door, *Win The Moment.* Or a note on your mirror that says: *Look in the mirror. That's your competition.* Run your own race and change the opponent.

3. **Strive Together:**
   When do you run faster, by yourself, or with someone else? With someone else. We need people to push us to be our best. Kevin Durant didn't go to the gym by himself when he was at Texas. He brought his teammates with him. That's what it looks like to strive together. Make a rule with yourself—don't go to practice without calling a teammate. (It's up to them to take you up on your offer.)

4. **Partner Up (Internally):**
   Your teammates are your teammates. Lift them up. Partner up with a teammate that plays the same position as you. Have a conversation with them about how you can view your relationship as a partnership. Support one another and encourage each other to bring your best effort every day in order to challenge one another.

   Example: a tennis coach encourages his players to lift up the player that they are playing against if they mess-up. The goal: if you can lift them up, they'll player better, and they will challenge you more.

5. **Partner Up (Externally):**
   Choose healthy competition over rivalry-based competition. When you're in a rivalry-based competition, it's impossible to be your best self. It becomes a cancer. Choose healthy competition by appreciating your competitors. If there's a player you're compared to individually, write him or her a thank-you note. Fuel yourself off positive emotion.

*Important: The only person you can control in this equation is **you**. Your coach or teammate might not view it this way—that shouldn't affect how you view it.*

Back to Kenny:

After covering the performance skills that Kenny wanted to work on, I asked him, "So your performance skills are what? They are the skills that make you a great...?"

He responded, "Performer."

Me: What are your moral character skills?

Kenny: The skills that make you a great teammate and a great friend.

Me: Which skills are more important to you?

Kenny: That's tough.

It is tough for Kenny. In a world where we're asked, "Did you win?" and "How many points did you score?" there are a lot of forces that get in the way of you being a great teammate and a great friend, which ultimately hurts the team—which ultimately hurts you.

We started to explore what it looks like to be a good teammate.

MORAL

- [x] Unselfish
- [x] Encouraging
- [x] Appreciative
- [x] Trustworthy
- [x] Caring

✔ Unselfish

I asked Kenny, "When someone hits a shot, scores a goal, or makes an acrobatic catch—what does the crowd do?"

Kenny: They cheer.

Me: When the crowd cheers—what are they expressing?

Kenny: Their approval.

Me: Have you ever got a standing ovation for getting your teammate a water?

Kenny: (Laughing) No.

Me: You've been conditioned to value performance over being a great teammate—why wouldn't you value the same thing?

Kenny: That's crazy man. I've never really thought about it like that before. It's like we're chasing the applause.

Pay For Points

I had a player call me and say, "Brett, I have an issue with my teammate. They're playing selfish and it's hurting our team."

I asked, "Why do you say that?"

The player responded, "Their parents are paying them for points."

That's a tough situation—you can't blame the player (who's getting paid) in this situation. The parents started the process (maybe with good intentions) of the player becoming selfish.

We asked our Academy, "What signal does it send to the player when his parents pay him for points?"

My favorite answer came from a seventh grader. Who said, "Don't pass."

I think that pretty much sums it up.

What will that player value? Scoring over everything. Why? There's a financial reward that supports the thought process. Why wouldn't he value that?

A Tough Question

Would you rather:

> Option 1: Win and score 5 points
> Option 2: Lose and score 30 points

Is there a right answer? That's not what I'm interested in. I'm interested in the honest answer, and if the right answer is the honest answer, that's great.

This would have been an easy question for me. I'm picking Option 2—every time.

Can I explain my logic? Here's an actual headline from a newspaper:

Ledbetter's 42 points wasn't enough.

When my friends read that, do you think they were thinking about the fact that we lost? Nope. What were they thinking? They were like, "Dude, you had 42 points?"

Lets think about this for a second. Let's use that same game for this example. Let's say I only had five points that game, and we win. Do you think that I'm making the headline? Nope.

And if they do mention me, what would it say? *Ledbetter was held to 5 points.* Then what do you think my friends are asking me? They're asking, "What's wrong man?" (Even though we won.)

Do you see where I'm coming from? I learned something at an early age. When you score a lot of points, what happens? You get a lot of attention. You know what I learned about that attention? It's easy to like it. It feels great.

Here's the thing: Blakely's in a very similar position that I was in. She's a prolific scorer in soccer and that's what everyone around her is constantly grading her on.

Blakely's Answer

I asked her an equivalent question for soccer.

Would you rather:

Option 1: Win and not score
Option 2: Lose and have three goals

Blakely's response was well thought out. She said, "In the regular season...I'd choose the loss and the hat trick. But in the post season (where it's win or go home) I'd choose the win."

Do you remember back to Part I? Do you remember the text conversation that she had?

Coach: Win? Score?

Blakely: 3 0. We played great.

Coach: Did you score?

Blakely: No.

Coach: What happened?

Why wouldn't Blakely value scoring goals over winning? The people around her infer that something is wrong when she doesn't score. She is sent very strong signals that scoring is what matters most. I experienced a lot of those strong forces.

Forces From the Outside

When I was a senior in high school, there were a few games where I really scored the ball. Here's an example of a headline:

Ledbetter Scores 49 to Help the Warriors win.

I remember after that game I didn't get a chance to talk with my dad at the gym. When I came home that night, I walked in and he was in the kitchen, eating. I took my shoes off and I asked him, "What'd you think of the game?" (I was expecting some praise.)

Instead, he said, "You're never going to win a championship like that."

He was right. It wasn't a team effort. I was getting in the way of that. Deep down inside, I knew that and here was the man who I looked up to the most telling me what I knew to be true. Yet I still didn't listen to him.

The outside forces were too seductive for me. I enjoyed the recognition and social status that came with the individual performances that I was stringing together. I was a conditional winner. I wanted our team to win, but that was my second priority.

What was my first? Me. That's why I picked lose and score 30. How does that impact team chemistry?

Making My Job Easier

I'm embarrassed to tell this story, but for the sake of learning I shared this with our Academy.

During a summer league game, between my sophomore and junior year, I was playing really well. Four seniors approached me after one of the games and said, "We're tired of playing with you. You don't pass us the ball. Next game, we are just going to stay on the defensive end. You can go 1 on 5."

My response, "Thanks, you're making my job easier."

It's embarrassing for me to admit that, but it gives you some insight into just how difficult of a person I became. Is it any wonder why we didn't have good player-to-player relationships?

If my teammates could have a choice between these two options to describe me, which would they have picked? Would they say I was Mr. Me? Or Mr. Team? Mr. Me.

In my mind, I was on a hunt. I was from a small town and I thought that having great stats was how you got scholarships. Scoring became an obsession. After leading the state of Missouri in scoring with a winning team—I realized that wasn't the case. I had no offers. More importantly, I didn't have any meaningful connections with my teammates.

The Unselfish Scorer

The question becomes: Is it possible to be an unselfish scorer? Is there such a thing? If so, who would you pick as an example?

Here's my vote: Kevin Durant.

Kevin is one of the best scorers the game of basketball has ever seen. Which is impressive. What's more impressive? I've *never* heard anybody say that Kevin is selfish.

Why is that?

Think back to the competitive section. Here's what Kevin Durant said:

One thing I try not to do is be a guy that goes into the gym and wants to be the only guy in the gym. I don't want to be the guy that says "I was working today, what were you doing?" I want to pull my teammates into the gym with me. If I work hard and we all work hard, I know only good things can come out of it.

Kevin *sends signals* to everybody around him that the team is his number one priority. Yet he still led the NBA in scoring multiple years.

I Want More

I was talking with a good friend of mine about how fragile teams are. He illustrated the point in an excellent way. Let's say you have 14 players on a (basketball) team. See if you agree with this:

> Players 9–14 want: to play
> Players 6–8 want: to start
> Players 4–5 want: more shots
> Players 2–3 want: to be the best player
> The best player wants: to play at the next level

What does this show? It's human nature to want more. There's nothing wrong with that.

Here's when it becomes an issue: when the feeling of wanting more outweighs what the team needs. To illustrate this point: everybody has to make sacrifices for a team to be successful. The coach asked his players a few questions. Every player got a sheet of paper with these questions on it:

1. How many minutes will you average?

The maximum amount of minutes a coach has to hand out in a basketball game is 200 minutes (5 players on court x 40-minute game). When this coach added his players' answers up it equaled 300 minutes. That's a game-and-a-half worth of minutes. *That's impossible.*

2. Will you start?

Basketball teams have five starters. This team had 9 starters. (Once again, impossible.)

3. How many points will you average?

According to expectations, this team would average 157 points. (That would be a record-setting number.)

What's this coach just done? He's undressed the truth. He's shown his team that sacrifices will have to be made.

Embracing Your Role

James Harden is an Olympic gold medalist and an NBA All-Star who's had an interesting path. When he came into the NBA, he had been the number-one option on *every* team that he'd ever played on. The Oklahoma City Thunder drafted him, and for the first three years in the NBA he didn't start. He came off the bench as the sixth man.

I asked James, "How hard was that transition?"

He said, "It's definitely a difficult challenge, especially in the beginning for me. My first two years were difficult getting adjusted to it."

As he talked more about it, it became apparent that he started to embrace his role. He explained his mindset as, "Having that mindset before I check in the game to change the game."

Why is this significant? James won the 6ᵗʰ man award in the NBA. He was then traded to the Houston Rockets and became a starter. His first game in Houston he had 45 points. What does this show? He is fully capable of scoring at a very high clip.

James knew that all along. That's why it's interesting to me that he accepted and embraced his role of being the sixth man. It was best for the team for him to buy in and do that job to the best of his ability. He did. If James didn't buy into his role, do you see how that could have created dysfunction within the team? That's what it looks like to be unselfish.

Side note: When is the best time to change your role—in-season or off-season? Change your role during the off-season by getting better. Embrace your role during the season by performing within it to the best of your ability.

Bad Player-to-Player Relationships

Why do bad player-to-player relationships happen? We asked our Academy and here were the 4 most common answers:

- Bad communication
- Jealousy
- Personal dislikes
- Different common goals

What do all of these things have in common? This is a bold statement, but I believe it to be true to my core. Anytime there's a player-to-player issue, it means one thing:

At least one of the players involved cares more about the back of the jersey than they do the front of the jersey.

What's on the back?
Your individual name or number.

What's on the front of the jersey?
The team.

When a player cares more about themselves than they do the team—that's when issues arise. Here's the hard thing: that's human nature.

Which is why it's so important to "play for the front of the jersey."

Dwayne Wade

Put yourself in this room: Team USA is having a meeting when Dwayne Wade stands up and says something to the whole team. Mike Krzyzewski tells the story:

Dwayne just said "Remember guys, we're playing for the three letters on the front of our jersey. USA. Not the name on the back."

Mike Krzyzewski, Basketball Coach,
Duke University

Nike got wind of the meeting and they designed the jerseys in a certain way based on what Dwayne said—take a look:

Check out the back. Do you see how they made the names the same color as the rest of the uniform? I love this design because it's an illustration of why I like to use the word unselfish versus the word selfless. Unselfish is less intense. *When you are unselfish your development still matters but the reason it matters is because you are plugging your talents into the team.*

I think the design of these jerseys captures this point perfectly. The USA (team) logo is in bold and has graphic dominance over the last name, which is subdued. But in the end, they both matter.

Body Language

I was having a conversation with a player about a game. I asked him to put himself in this situation:

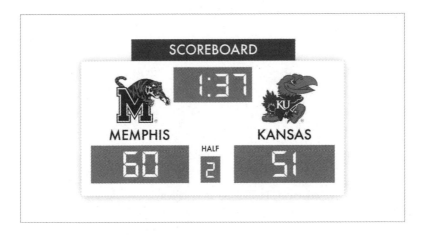

Me: If you're on Kansas' team, if you're being honest, what are most people thinking in this situation—positive or negative thoughts?

Player: Negative.

Me: Let's say you aren't like most people and you are thinking positive thoughts. But I'm your teammate and I'm thinking negative thoughts. If you see me down and you're a good teammate, what are you going to do?

Player: Lift you up.

Me: When you do that, who's your focus on?

Player: You.

Me: Who's it not on?

Player: The team.

Do you see how body language can get in the way of what's best for the team?

The example from above was from the 2008 national championship game. That actually happened. Kansas ended up coming back and winning the game. It was amazing because their body language never changed; it stayed positive. I asked Bill Self, the head basketball coach for the University of Kansas, about the importance of body language and he said, "That night if body language had changed, the game is over."

Bench Cam

I ask players, "Do you like being subbed out?" I've never met a player that answers "yes" to that question. That being said, I love paying attention to how they exit the game and enter the bench. That's why Becky Burleigh and I film the bench at the University of Florida.

Here are a few things that we look for:

What's the exchange like when your teammate is coming in for you? Once you get to the bench, do you give energy? Or do you take energy? Do you go to the end of the bench and disconnect because you are frustrated? There are a lot of selfish signals that can be sent in this situation.

Here's an example: one of Becky's players is coming out of the game. Becky talks with every player that comes out of the game to get on the same page. In this situation, a player (let's call her Kacey) comes out of the game. Kacey holds herself to a high standard and when she doesn't meet that standard, she becomes frustrated.

That's exactly what happened in this situation. Kacey comes out of the game, talks with Becky and walks in front of her teammates on the bench and gives them half-hearted, not making eye-contact, high-fives.

To say it's not good and useful thinking is an understatement. The bench cam is positioned at the end of the bench. Kacey continues to walk out of the frame (which is complete disconnection from the team) and shows frustration.

In soccer, you have to wear pennies when you are on the bench. Kacey comes back into the frame to grab her penny. Once she gets it, she then walks back out of the frame. Once she's back out of the frame, her teammate notices her away from the team spiraling in a downward direction.

Her teammate then walks over to console Kacey and get her back on track. Three minutes later, they walk back in the frame and Kacey is encouraging from the bench. Becky brought Kacey into the office the next day to address this. (The only time we would show negative body language from the bench cam would be in an individual meeting.)

Becky said, "When your teammate, who hasn't even gotten in the game yet, has to come over to help you out for three minutes, what signal does that send?"

Kacey, tearing up, said, "It's selfish."

The clip shook Kacey and it changed her behavior. She became much more aware of how she exited the game and encouraged her teammates.

Selfish Signals

Players are constantly sending signals. Those signals are shaping what your teammates think about you. Ask your teammates (or self-reflect) and think about the signals that you are sending. Would they line up with what's best for the team? Here are a few for you to consider:

Action:
Not confronting a difficult teammate who is doing something to harm the team.

Signal:
Personal feelings > Team

Action:
Passing up a shot in a clutch situation (when you're the best option) because you don't want your teammates to think you're a ball hog.

Signal:
Personal feelings > Team

Action:
You are visibly upset after having a bad individual performance despite the team winning.

Signal:
Me > Team

Examine your signals. Would your teammates (or coach) think that you are selfish or unselfish?

5 Ways to Exercise Unselfishness

1. **Recognize Outside Forces:**
    Pay attention to the questions that you are getting asked after games. Who are the people that ask the questions that undermine what you are trying to do with your team? What are the questions that they ask? Think back to Blakely: After winning 3–0, what did her coach ask her after he realized that she didn't have one of those goals? He asked, "What happened?"

    Disconnect from the forces that are seductive and cause you to think about yourself first. Find ways to insulate yourself with things that will help you maintain clarity on what's really important—being a great player and a great teammate.

2. **Create a filter: What's best for the team?**
    Before making decisions that affect the team, ask yourself: What's best for the team? When you are mindful of how your actions affect the team, you begin to make decisions based on what can help the team. When your actions reflect what you feel is best for the team—you are projecting unselfishness.

    When people ask those who know Kevin Durant, "How is he?" Nobody says anything negative. That's a hard thing to do as a scorer who's led the NBA in scoring multiple times. Why is he able to do it? He does what's best for the team.

3. **Embrace Your Role:**
    On teams, sacrifices have to be made. Think back to the typical team. *Everyone wants more.* The questions

the coach asked his players proved that. James Harden embraced his role by doing it to the best of his ability. Could he have done more? In his mind, "Of course."

Remember, if you aren't satisfied with your role, the time to change it is in the off-season. In-season, embrace your role to the best of your ability.

4. **Body Language:**
   Your body language tells a story. What story are you telling? Does your body language support a team-first mentality? When you come out of the game, how do you exit the game? When you are on the bench, do you encourage your teammates?

5. **Ask your coach: "Do I send selfish signals?"**
   Self reflect. Or ask your teammate or your coach, "Do I send any selfish signals?" Remember, your teammates don't base their friendships on your athletic achievement. They base it on who you are as a person. Make sure your signals line up with who you want to be and how you want to be talked about.

☑ Encouraging

I asked Kenny, "Can you think of a situation where you were really struggling and somebody helped you out?"

He said, "Yep."

Me: Who helped you and what did they say?

Kenny: (Pausing) His name was Neil. He was very influential in my life. I was at a really low place and he took me aside and said, "I believe in you."

Me: How did that make you feel?

Kenny: (Tearing up) It meant everything to me. He helped me hold it together.

Me: That's the power of encouragement. You have the ability to help others feel that same feeling.

What a Leader Looks Like

I was talking with a high-level coach and he said, "My point guard steals the confidence of his teammates by having negative body language."

I asked his permission to work with his player.

The first thing I asked the player (let's call him Marcus) was, "What do you think the primary responsibility of a point guard is?"

Marcus told me, "Be the coach on the floor."

That was a perfect answer. I knew exactly where we needed to go.

I showed him a clip of Sherri Coale. Sherri's the head women's basketball coach at the University of Oklahoma. I asked her the same question that I asked Marcus, "What is the primary responsibility of a point guard?"

Sherri Coale, Women's Basketball Coach, University of Oklahoma

The primary responsibility of a point guard is to deal hope. Your job is to make everyone around you believe that anything is possible all the time. You can't do that if your shoulders are slumped, if your head is down, or if you look grouchy. You absolutely can't deal hope if you look that way.

The number one job of a point guard (coach on the floor) is to deal hope.

I asked Marcus, "What do you think about what Sherri said?"

He responded, "That's right on."

Choose: 0% Or 50%

After that, I showed Marcus a clip of Jack Clark, the rugby coach at the University of California, Berkeley. Marcus had no idea who Jack was. After I explained to him that Jack has won over 20 national championships and has a 90% winning percentage, he perked up. I showed him a video clip of an interview that I did with Jack. Here's what Jack said:

For the first fifteen years that I coached, if we were having a bad training session…I would circle the team up and give them the business and then send them back out. It never once got better.

Jack Clark, Rugby Coach, University of California, Berkeley

Now I just find a way to find something positive. A guy passes the ball and the other guy drops it. I say, "Good pass." It drives me crazy in a way…but I force myself to find something positive. About half the time I can draw a team out of that funk and get back on track—playing to our abilities.

When Jack goes negative, it gets better 0% of the time.

When Jack stays positive, it gets better 50% of the time.

That makes a lot of sense to me. If I missed six shots in a row and a coach piles it on (by yelling), I'm not sure that would help me. Marcus agreed.

I asked him, "So you agree with Jack's statement? It doesn't get better when you go negative?"

Marcus: Yes.

Me: If you agree with that statement, when is it acceptable to go negative?

Marcus: I guess, never.

The previous day Marcus told me that he struggled with being positive. (His thoughts: 80% negative/20% positive.) He started to understand that he really needed to change his inner dialogue if he was going to be able to deal encouragement to his teammates.

Where Does the "Next-Play Mentality" Come From?

We then started to talk about "The Next-Play Mentality." I asked Marcus if he knew who Geno Auriemma was. He knew that Geno coached basketball at the University of Connecticut and was on his way to becoming the most successful coach in the history of the women's game.

I showed him a video clip—I asked Geno, "Where does a Next-Play Mentality come from?"

You know where that comes from? It comes from your coaches. There are a lot of coaches (me included) we're hoarders. We hoard bad plays. I've found that when I let plays go and move on to the next play, my players do too.

Geno Auriemma, Women's Basketball Coach, University of Connecticut

I asked Marcus, "What do you think about Geno's statement?"

He told me, "I agree 100 percent. My teammate gets frustrated easily. Last night, when he missed a shot the coach said, 'That's a great look. Keep shooting.' My teammate got over it quick and moved to the next play faster."

Me: How does that apply to you?

Marcus: I can do that for my teammates. I can make part of my job to help my teammates get to the next play.

The Most Important Three Seconds

One of my favorite clips to show players features LeBron James on a fast break. In this clip, LeBron is double-teamed by the defense, which opens up a lane for his teammate to cut and get a layup. LeBron throws the ball to where he thinks his teammate should go. His teammate doesn't go. The ball goes out of bounds and is turned over to the other team.

LeBron piles it on his teammate by yelling at him for not cutting to the basket. What do you think happens? His teammate gets defensive and they start arguing in a post-season game on national TV. In that moment, LeBron's frustration got the best of him and he gave his teammate a verbal onslaught.

It's important to note that one moment doesn't define anybody. This moment is not indicative of who LeBron is—it's a great teachable moment that helps players understand what going negative looks like, and how it prevents people from moving to the next play. The question becomes: How do you help move people to the next play?

Here's what I've found with players: when they mess up, they look around. What they see in those next three seconds is very important. In fact, we call it *the most important three seconds.* If they look around and see someone express disappointment, that can have a negative impact on the person moving forward.

As a teammate (or coach), in those three seconds, you can do one of two things to help the player that just made a mistake. You can:

1. Confirm they messed up.
2. Build them up.

Players who manage the first few seconds after making a mistake (the best) are typically the most resilient. When mistakes are met with support instead of judgment, teams take off. We illustrated this point to the University of Florida's soccer team by walking into the film room and showing the team clips of every single mistake that was made from the previous game.

We then asked the team—what'd you guys see?

They talked about it in their groups and they tried to put a positive spin on it, "We have a lot of room to improve—our best play is ahead of us."

We acknowledged that was a great point. But then we said, "What did every clip have in common?"

They responded, "They were all of our mistakes."

We then said, "You know what we saw that every one of the clips had in common?"

Curious, they asked, "What?"

"Every one of the clips was of you guys making mistakes—not one time did we see a negative reaction to a mistake. You guys met each other with support. That's what makes us different."

When you have a group of people helping each other move to the next play by building each other up, that's special.

Best Teammate Ever

I asked Marcus, "Do you know who DeAndre Jordan is?"

He said, "Yeah. He had 27 rebounds the other night."

DeAndre is an NBA player who is frequently on ESPN SportsCenter's Top-10 Plays because of his ability to dunk on people. I had the opportunity to interview DeAndre and ask him a tough question. I shared the conversation with Marcus:

Me: Who's the best teammate you ever played with? What was his best quality?

DeAndre: Now all my teammates aren't going to want to hang out with me.

Me: Somebody popped into your head.

DeAndre: You're right. Chauncey Billups. There were times when I'd get frustrated and he wouldn't even say anything because we had a lot of talks throughout the season. He would just look at me and…(DeAndre gestures: he taps his temples, on both sides of his head, with both index fingers.) And I'm like, "OK. That's over." (Chauncey) didn't even have to say anything. I knew I had to forget about what happened and lock back into the game.

You know what's cool? Think about how many teams DeAndre has been on. Whether you know who Chauncey Billups is or not, what separated him in DeAndre's mind? He helped him reset in difficult times.

I showed Marcus this and asked him, "What do you think about that?"

He said, "I want my teammates to say that about me."

We began to talk about how he could do that.

Opportunities For Encouragement

The definition we use for the word encouraging is:

Encouraging: Dealing confidence and support.

I was talking with Marcus and I asked him, "When do people need encouragement the most?"

He responded, "When things are going badly for them."

Me: What are some of the opportunities that basketball provides for you to be encouraging with your teammates?

Marcus named off a few examples:

- A coach yelling at them
- Right after they've made a mistake
- Missing shots
- Bad calls

We started to see how many ways he could connect with his teammates like Chauncey Billups connected with DeAndre Jordan. He was going to become their reset button by helping them replace their negative thoughts with positive thoughts.

Replace Negative

Do you remember back to the Positive section? One of the most common questions that I get asked is, "When I go negative, how do I get back to being positive?" There are three steps:

1. Acknowledge the thought.
2. Interrupt the thought.
3. Replace the thought.

Not only is this how you get back to positive, these three steps can also help you get a teammate back to positive. See below:

1. Acknowledge your teammate who is struggling.
2. Interrupt your teammate's negative thought process.
3. Replace your teammate's thought with a good and useful thought.

The only way that you can acknowledge that your teammate is struggling is to get outside of yourself and pay attention to your teammate. What does that look like?

I used one of Marcus' examples that he gave me to teach a point. I asked him, "Picture your teammate getting yelled at by your coach. You got that?"

Marcus: Yep. My coach calls him "soft."

Me: What would he be thinking in that situation?

Marcus: He gets embarrassed.

Me: How could you interrupt and replace that thought?

Marcus: I can tell him, "Don't give in. Bounce back—you got this." I'd let him know that I have his back.

It comes down to you getting to know what works for your teammates and delivering that message to them. Chauncey Billups knew what worked for DeAndre. Find out how to acknowledge that your teammate is struggling and interrupt the negative thought process by replacing it with something positive.

Encouraging Texts

Think back to the Resilient section: Do you remember when Blakely missed the shootout penalty kick to lose in the first round of the conference tournament that her team was favored to win? That was a tough moment for her. The only loss that could be worse than that is a season-ending loss in the NCAA Tournament.

How would you feel if you missed the opportunity to win the game?

This was the lowest point for Blakely (and her team) of the season. As much as this moment hurt her, it was a great opportunity for her to see the support system that she had within their team. After the game she received a text message from every one of her teammates. Everybody on her team had her back.

We talked about how much it meant to her. I asked her, "How'd that make you feel?"

Blakely: (Tearing up) It meant a lot.

Me: Imagine if you used your talent (she's an extremely talented player) to give others that feeling by encouraging them in their time of need?

Blakely: I will. This has been a great lesson for me.

I told Marcus that story and he said, "Man, I need to step my game up."

Teammate Day

Marcus was talking to me about the transition to college. He said, "You don't really think about it when you're in high school, but it's a tough transition. A lot of us are the best in our school, state, and maybe even country. When you get to school, you realize the other 12 guys on your team were the exact same as you. The only difference now is they're four years older than you."

Me: Do you remember somebody helping you through the first year?

Marcus: That first year was rough. The guy I was playing behind really helped me through the "Am I good enough to be here?" time.

Me: How did that make you feel?

Marcus: His support is what got me through. It was important.

We started to talk about the current team. I asked, "Who's struggling right now?"

He said, "One of our freshmen."

Me: He's going to have a great practice today, you know why?

Marcus: Why?

Me: You have one job—to make sure you lift him up and help him have a great practice. How do you think that will make him feel?

Marcus: He's going to be like, "He's helping me a lot today." (Smiling) He'll feel important, though, like I have his back.

We call it "Teammate Day." If someone is struggling and needs to get on track, it's a great tool to assist with that. Here's another one.

Catch Them Doing It Right

This is the most effective strategy I've found with giving feedback to players. Coach K uses it with his players, and I think players can use this with their teammates. He told me:

We as coaches can always catch a kid doing something wrong and we overlook the things that they are doing right. They'll do less wrong things if we catch the right things. A right thing is not just hitting a bucket.

Mike Krzyzewski, Basketball Coach, Duke University

Here are a few examples that he gave me:

- Saying something that is encouraging to a teammate.
- Being smart in a certain situation.
- Helping a teammate.

He then said, "Point out winning plays."

Think back to what Jack Clark said at the beginning of this section. He said that when he goes negative it gets better 0% of the time. Coach K's strategy helps you stay on the positive side of the equation. Can we agree that, in some environments it's difficult to stay positive?

To prove this point, here's a conversation that I had with Marcus:

I asked him, "If your first team plays your second team in practice, which team should win?"

Marcus: The first team.

Me: What's more likely to happen? If the second team beats your first team—your coach praising the second team, or your coach yelling at your first team?

Marcus: (Laughing) Yelling at the first team.

Me: What signal does that send to the second team?

Marcus: That he only cares about the first team and the people on the second team don't matter.

Think about that for a second. In this situation, the coach has a choice. He can go negative with the first team, or he can encourage the second team to continue to challenge and play well. If you're in an environment where this is the case, it's critical for you as a player to counterbalance the negative energy by being encouraging to your teammates.

Bench Cam

You know how you can tell how encouraging a team is? You can tell by watching their bench. I asked Marcus, "Would you rather sit or play?"

He looked at me like *is this a real question?* He said, "Play."

That's my point. I've never met a player who would rather sit than play. When you see someone supporting another when it comes at the expense of them playing—that's inspiring. Marcus agreed.

I showed him a clip of an interview that I did with Brad Stevens, who is currently coaching in the NBA:

Brad Stevens, NBA Coach,
Boston Celtics

One of the things that we do is we show bench clips all the time. We show our bench cheering. We show them going crazy. I don't mind if they get told to sit down (by the refs)—I think that's a really good thing. I want them to be engaged in the game, and the best teams we've had have been.

I think as a coach you try to spend as much time with guys 8–14 on your roster as you do 1–7. Those guys at 8–14 need to know how much you care about them. And they need to know how important they are to your collective success.

There are two things I took away from what Brad Stevens said:

1. He films his bench.
2. He spends just as much time with players 8–14 as he does with 1–7.

That hits me hard because I never played for a coach who did either one of those things. I started to ask other coaches how they coached their bench. Here's what Coach K told me:

Mike Krzyzewski, Basketball Coach,
Duke University

We've always taped our bench. I tape my bench a lot—not for negative stuff. Sometimes the guy who's a starter, who plays 39 of the 40 minutes, never realizes the support he gets from the bench.

Imagine sitting in your film room watching film with a split screen. On the left side of the screen is the bench. On the right side of the screen is the live game. They're in sync. So as the game plays, you can see the reaction of the bench. How cool would it be for the players playing to see the bench's reaction to their performance?

I mean seriously, think about what you would think if you saw your team explode in excitement because of something that you did. How would that make you feel?

Or, on the flipside, let's say you make a mistake. How would it make you feel if the person who played the same position (and wants to play) is supporting you through it all and rooting you on? Do you see how powerful that could be?

It makes sense why these coaches film their bench. It's a great way to show your team what the word encouraging looks like in action.

Marcus gained an appreciation for the bench. He couldn't believe how much attention these coaches spent on building the encouragement levels on the bench. His feeling was, "My coach would never film our bench."

I asked him, "What can you take away from this?"

He said, "I can be mindful of how I'm supporting my guys from the bench. I never realized how much it can help—instead of being frustrated by coming out, I'm going to be an encourager."

Reminder: "Play Green"

As we've covered in a previous section, the soccer team at the University of Florida films their bench. Leading up to the Elite 8 game (where they played Stanford) we built a lot of messages around going all-in. We asked the players to think of a stoplight. If yellow is playing cautious, we wanted to encourage them to "Play Green!" Everybody wore green wristbands as a visual reminder.

Stanford was a tough matchup. They had only given up two goals the entire year on their field. (They scored 34.) Anytime they scored, they felt like they were in control because of how good they were defensively.

In the first five minutes of this game, Stanford scores. What happened next was inspiring. For most teams the thought might be, "We're in trouble." The bench cam captured our reaction. One of the senior leaders turned to the rest of the team and yells, "This is where we are louder than ever."

After she yelled that, the team then held up their green wristbands to the 11 players on the field. Talk about support. Within a few minutes the score was tied. To see that kind of support from the bench in the most pressurized situation was amazing.

It makes sense why Muffet McGraw, who is a championship coach that leads the women's basketball program at The University of Notre Dame, told me, "I think your team attitude is often the result of the last players on your bench."

5 Ways to Exercise Encouragement

1. **Replace Negative:**
   How did Chauncey Billups reset DeAndre Jordan?

They had a reset cue. Chauncey would point to his temple and that helped DeAndre forget about what happened and pull him into the present. How do you do that with your teammates?

Replace the negative thoughts of your teammates with these three steps: Acknowledge, Interrupt, Replace. Find out how to acknowledge that your teammate is struggling, interrupt the negative thought process, and replace it with something positive.

2. **Catch Them Doing Something Right:**
   Jack Clark said when he goes negative, the situation gets better 0% of the time. When he goes positive, it gets better 50% of the time. How do you stay positive? Catch people doing something right. Identify things that you can point out to your teammates to encourage them to repeat it. Challenge yourself to catch something from each one of your teammates every day in practice.

3. **Teammate Day:**
   Get outside of yourself and help your teammate get back on track. Pay attention to who's struggling and make your goal the next day in practice to partner with that person (without him or her knowing) to help your teammate have a great practice.

4. **Encouraging Text:**
   Think back to a time where you were struggling and somebody sent you something that lifted your spirits. How did that make you feel? Why not give others that same feeling? Identify times when you can support your teammates. If somebody is struggling shoot him or her

a text saying: *Let's go to practice early tomorrow. I'll rebound for you.*

5. **Bench Clips:**

    We determined that almost every player would rather play than sit. That's why it means so much to see teammates supporting each other from the bench. Ask your coach to film the bench. If this isn't possible, pay attention to how you are when you are on the bench. Do you support your teammates? When you come out of the game, do you encourage the player coming in? Or do you express frustration? It takes a special person to be excited for another person's success, especially when it's at their expense.

☑ Trustworthy

I asked Kenny, "Do you want your teammates to consider you trustworthy?"

He said, "Yeah."

Me: What makes you trust someone?

Kenny: You can rely on them

Me: How do you build that?

Kenny: I don't know.

Me: You'll love this story.

Straightjacket

Billy Donovan, former men's basketball coach at the University of Florida, is a championship coach. I asked him, "Why is winning a championship important?" He told me, "The value comes in an understanding that anything in life, in my opinion, that's worth achieving cannot be done on your own."

That's a great thought.

But here's my thing, a lot of coaches have great thoughts. So for me, I'm always interested in seeing how they deliver the information to their players. What I'm *really* interested in is seeing how their players receive it.

Chandler Parsons, an NBA Player, played for Billy at Florida. I asked Chandler, "What was the best thing that you learned from Billy?"

He told me a story:

Chandler Parsons, NBA Player

Coach Donovan lined up all of us across half-court. He picked one player to basically step out in front of the team and he handed him a straightjacket. He put him in and tied him up and locked him in.

Then he was like, "Get out." I believe it was Vernon Macklin. He was trying to get out and was struggling and struggling and struggling. He couldn't do it and literally coach let this go on for like 5–10 minutes.

Finally, I just went for it. I just went and helped him and untied him and was like, "Here, now get out."

His whole thing was, "We can't do this by ourselves. We all have to help one another. Like Vernon is stuck right there in a straightjacket, Chandler stepped up and helped him out." I think that was huge for us throughout the rest of the season. We knew that we had to count on each other and we couldn't do anything individually.

That's big-time coaching right there. What did Chandler take away from Billy?

You cannot do anything on your own. To refresh, here's the last line of why Billy said championships are important:

Anything in life, in my opinion, that's worth achieving cannot be done on your own.

The Two Sides of Trust

Great relationships are built on trust. The question becomes: How do you build trust? Here's how we define that word at our Academy:

Trust: to rely on someone or something.

The straightjacket example illustrates perfectly how trust is built. Trust is built through codependency and there are two sides to trust. One side has to be trustworthy. One side has to be trustwilling.

1. Trustworthy: being reliable.
2. Trustwilling: relying on others.

When trustwilling and trustworthy intersect, that's where trust is built. In the straightjacket example, Vernon was stuck. He was in a position where he couldn't do it on his own.

When people are put in a position where they can't do it on their own they oftentimes become more trustwilling. That's why adversity can be a great thing. It helps you realize that you need to trust other people to accomplish great things.

Chandler stepped up for Vernon when he was trustwilling. By doing so he proved that in that moment he was trustworthy. The more moments they string together like that, the stronger the bond of trust becomes.

Trust is built when trustwilling meets trustworthy. When that consistently happens—a strong form of trust is built.

Tied Up

Here's a fun exercise to illustrate to a team what trust looks like at a meal. All you need is string, food, and a team. The string is used to tie everybody's wrist together.

You then sit the team in a circle (or a big rectangle) and together they eat a meal with their hands tied together. As you can imagine it gets a little complicated when they have to use utensils to cut. The only way it can work is if everybody works together to help each other eat. It's a great way to illustrate what trust looks like in something that you already do as a team. After the team finishes, the group then discusses how this illustrates trust.

Rhonda Faehn asked me to do this exercise with her team when she was the head gymnastics coach at the University of

Florida. At the time, they were coming off of back-to-back national championships.

Their message: we are dependent on each other to accomplish our team goals. Trust is built every day and every day that we practice, we prove to our teammates and coaches that we are worthy of their trust.

Fast forward four months, after they won their third straight national championship, one of their players said in the post-game interview, "I've always said, if your coach trusts you, then there's nothing that should stop you. Rhonda 100% trusts every one of us athletes. And you can see that. Before beam she's not over there in our face saying 'You gotta do this.' She's over there like, 'Have fun. Go out there and do exactly what we've been training to do.'"

How cool is that? Here's another example on how we illustrated what trust looks like to two of the players on the University of Florida's soccer team.

Breath Share

Have you ever been on a team where you and another player weren't always on the same page? Everybody has, right? There were two players that I worked with in that situation. It's not that they didn't get along, it's just they weren't ever going to sit together at team meals because they didn't naturally connect and would have to work for conversation.

We needed to fix that by increasing their connection to one another because they play positions on the field where they interact often. I got in touch with the coach (and one of my partners in crime) Becky Burleigh. We called the girls and had them meet us at the pool. They had no idea what we were doing.

When they got to the pool, we gave them flippers and *one* snorkel.

The objective: they had to swim the full length of the pool (sharing the snorkel) without bringing their heads above water to breathe.

There are a few things that made this difficult. When they passed the snorkel underwater, water got in it. They had to *clear the snorkel* by blowing the water out of it before they could breathe in. If they didn't, they would swallow a bunch or chlorine. That's exactly what happened on their first time.

They realized very quickly that they had to find a way to work together to accomplish the task. They were put in a situation where they had to rely on each other for breath. They figured it out and got better each time.

Here's what made it all worth it. The soccer team played a few days later. One of the two scores a goal. After the goal, a photographer captured a picture of them hugging. That would have never happened if we didn't pour our energy into putting them in shared experiences where they had to depend on each other.

One of the players sent me a text of the picture the following morning. I said, "You have to send that to her."

She said, "She already sent it to me."

We won that day.

Two Types of People

I was having a conversation with Napheesa, who is a high-level basketball player we talked with in Part I, about trust. I asked her, "What makes you trust someone?"

She responded, "I trust people until they give me a reason not to."

Me: That's interesting.

Napheesa: I think there are two types of people. There are people who trust others until they give them a reason not to, and there are people who don't trust anybody until that trust is earned.

Me: That's a pretty profound statement.

Napheesa: (Laughs)

I think there's a lot of truth to what she said. The key to gaining (and keeping) access to others' trust is being consistent. If you want to be considered trustworthy by your teammates, you need to fully understand what goes into that. Here are a few strategies for you to become more trustworthy with your teammates and coaches.

One Man Down

Sport is such a great platform to teach trust. A football coach wanted to show his team what it looks like to be trustworthy. There was an offensive lineman who wasn't doing his job. He wasn't protecting the quarterback the way he should. During a scrimmage the coach called the lineman over to him.

He then said to the team, "Keep scrimmaging."

The offensive team was now at a disadvantage. By removing one of the linemen, the offensive team was put in a situation where they had one fewer man blocking. Now, one of the defensive linemen had a clear path to the quarterback without being blocked. As the ball was hiked and the quarterback dropped back, the defensive lineman charged straight at the quarterback without being blocked and lit him up.

As that happened the coach turned to the offensive lineman on the sideline and said, "That's what it feels like to play with you."

The team was relying on this player to do his job and he wasn't. The coach wanted to illustrate to him how much the team depended on him. The team was trustwilling. He needed to prove that he was trustworthy. The best way he could do that was to fulfill his role.

Words = Actions

Do you want your teammates to consider you trustworthy? Then your words should meet your actions. When your words and actions meet that sends a signal: *I'm reliable*. On the flip side, when your words don't equal your actions, what happens? You appear unreliable. Consider these two examples:

1. A teammate trusts you with information that they don't want anybody else to know. They ask you to keep it between you and them. You agree and say, "I won't tell anybody." A few days later, a different teammate brings up the teammate's (who trusted you) situation. You share with them what they told you. It then spreads back to the person.

    Words: I won't tell anybody.
    Actions: you tell a teammate.
    Signal: unreliable.

2. In a team meeting, everybody decides to not cosign (seen in the Courage section) on actions that are harmful to the team. The coach asks, "Are we good with this?" Everybody responds, "Yes."

    Words: yes (agreement to not cosign).
    Actions: you don't confront a teammate for going out and drinking the night before a game.
    Signal: you aren't reliable.

Think of a time where you told a teammate something and did the opposite. Can you see why they might have thought you were unreliable? The accumulation of those signals leads to people not trusting you.

Look For the Straightjacket

The players in our basketball academy really love the straight-jacket example from Chandler Parsons. How do you recreate that? Here's what we do: each session in our academy we learn a new move.

If we see someone struggling with a new move we will say, "Derrick's in a straightjacket." What happens next is cool. You'll see one of Derrick's training teammates come over to help him.

As instructors at our academy when we see a player struggling we view it as an opportunity to build trust. A lot of coaches feel value by fixing the problem. We try and use that as an opportunity for teammates to build trust. The player struggling has to be trustwilling to accept the information from their teammate. The teammate teaching has to prove that her or she is trustworthy by delivering good information.

When those two things intersect we celebrate it because trust is being built. One teammate is proving that he or she is trust-worthy by helping a struggling teammate.

I asked a player, "How could you build trust like this?"

Player: look for opportunities when my teammates are strug-gling and invest in helping them.

Player-Led Practice

A high-level tennis coach told his best player (let's call him Wesley) on a Friday, "You are running the show on Monday." Wesley was the leader of this team and he had the weekend to plan practice for the team on Monday.

The coach bumped into Wesley on Monday morning and asked him, "You ready for the big day?"

Wesley was. Right before practice the coach asked him, "What do you need from me?" Wesley told him, "I need you to feed tennis balls to the guys during the drills and to keep time of the drills." Wesley gave him the itinerary.

I asked Wesley, "How'd practice go that day?"

He said, "It went great. I got a lot out of it. I think the guys liked it because it was fresh."

After practice the coach brought the team in and said, "Give Wesley a hand. Thank you for running practice."

What a brilliant move by the coach. He switched up the flow by letting a player lead practice. What has the coach done in this situation? He's put Wesley, the team leader, in a position where the others have to rely on him. Do you see how that would build trust?

Not only is this a great trust-builder. We do player-led instruction every session at our basketball academy. Here's an advantage that you can tell your coach to encourage him or her to try this. When we have our players lead instruction it frees us (the coach) up to watch and understand the dynamics of the group.

The coach doesn't have to waste any of their bullets with instruction. They can save their voice for really important things.

Here's what's cool. Back to Wesley, I asked his coach, "How similar was his practice to what you would have done?"

The coach smiled, "It was better."

I laughed.

He said, "Not only are you building trust within your team. But I trust them more. They've proved how trustworthy they are. It makes them a more enjoyable group to coach."

Could you try that with your coach?

Alternating Shots

College golf is tricky. It's an individual sport that's coded as a team sport. The sport itself offers a great way to build trust between players. Coaches can use the alternating shot style to help build the trust levels within their team.

Here's how it works. You are partnered with another golfer. One golfer will tee off. His partner will then have the next shot. Each shot they alternate. Do you see how the score is fully dependent on each other? If one hits a bad shot it puts the other in a tough position. Together they can prove to each other that they are trustworthy.

We took that idea into basketball. If there are two players that aren't completely getting along we use this exercise. Before each player can leave practice they have to hit six three-pointers in a row taking turns alternating shots. In other words, each of the players has to hit three three-pointers in a row.

As a player, how could you create codependency within your sport? I asked a tennis player that question. He said, "We do a rally-share. There are a certain number (say 150) of rallies we have to get in order to end practice."

Do you see how you and your coach could find ways to create a codependency challenge to help teammates that aren't fully cooperating? Think back to the snorkel breath share. It helps build trust by creating those experiences.

5 Ways to Exercise Trustworthiness

1. **Fulfill Your Role:**
   Your teammates depend on you to fill your role. Just like the offensive lineman, you have an obligation to your team to do your job to the best of your abilities. Work with your coach to fully understand your role. Use the job description as a way for you to prove that you're trustworthy to your teammates.

2. **Words = Actions:**
   When your words and your actions line up it sends a signal that you are reliable. The accumulation of those signals leads to trust. Build an awareness that helps you follow through with what you say you're going to do.

3. **Straightjacket:**
   Chandler Parsons helped his teammate out of a straight-jacket when he was struggling. Look at your teammates struggling as an opportunity to help them out and build trust. When you deliver good information in their times of need, you prove that you are trustworthy. The more moments you can prove that, the more they will trust you.

4. **Player-Led Instruction (or Practice):**
   Talk with your coach. Find ways inside of practice where the players can lead the instruction. This will free him or her up to see the group dynamics of how

the team interacts. Also, it will put players in a position where they have to rely on each other to learn and understand information.

5. **Codependency Challenges:**
   Take a lesson from college golf. Trust is built through codependency. Alternating shots is a great way to build that. Find ways inside your sport to create codependency challenges. For basketball we have players end practice by making six three-pointers alternating shots together. For tennis, you rally share. Talk with your coach—what are ways inside your sport that you can create a codependency challenge?

☑ Appreciative

I asked Kenny, "Have you ever heard a coach say, 'Enjoy the journey?'"

Kenny: Yeah.

Me: Do you struggle with that?

Kenny: Yeah.

Me: Why?

Kenny: I see all of these dreams inside my head and I worry about whether or not they'll come true.

Appreciation-to-Entitlement Ratio

Shaka Smart is the head basketball coach at the University of Texas. We share a similar belief around the importance of appreciation. I had a conversation with him about this character skill.

Me: What's the thing that your players hear you talk about the most?

Shaka: The thing I talk about most is appreciation. That's the number-one core value in our program. I feel like appreciation is the foundation for anyone that is successful over a long period of time, on or off the court.

He then went on to talk about a ratio that's really important to him:

Shaka: I believe in an appreciation-to-entitlement ratio. Appreciation should be high. Entitlement should be low. If someone feels like when they take the floor they deserve something because of who they are or because of what they've done, they automatically are not going to be in the right frame of mind to make their team win at the highest level.

Entitlement = Thinking you deserve something based on *who you are* or *what you've done.*

Appreciation: To recognize the good in someone or something.

How do we raise our levels of appreciation? Here are a few helpful strategies.

Those Points Don't Count

One of my favorite coaching moments came from watching Sherri Coale, the women's basketball coach at the University of Oklahoma. She was in day two of coaching the USA Basketball's world championship team—a team that was comprised of the best women college basketball players.

Her energy was incredible. The engagement level was amazing from the team. Fourteen out of fourteen women (I counted) had their eyes on her anytime that she addressed the team.

Kaleena Mosqueda-Lewis plays for the University of Connecticut. She's an excellent player, and a particularly great shooter. In fact, she's made the most three-point field goals in the history of Division I women's basketball. During a USA basketball team scrimmage, her University of Connecticut teammate, Bria Hartley, was on her team. I distinctly remember one play that involved both of them.

Kaleena came off a great screen and Bria delivered her a perfect pass. Kaleena shot it and knocked down the three. They started to retreat back to the other end to play defense. Before they could get set, Sherri stopped play.

She said to everybody, "Those points don't count."

She then addressed Kaleena, "Did you point to Bria for delivering you a great pass?"

Kaleena smiled and said, "My bad, coach. Great pass, Bria."

Think about that for a second. The result was great: the shot went in. The process was great: the team executed the play. Most people would be blinded by the result. Sherri wasn't.

What was Sherri coaching in that moment? She was coaching Kaleena (as a person) by creating a teachable moment to develop the character skill, Appreciation.

Talent wasn't going to be what this team lacked—they had a lot of it. How the team worked together was going to be critical—maybe even a difference maker further down the line—which is why Sherri was taking the time to coach appreciation.

A Moment That Changed My Life

I met with Tyler in a hotel lobby. It was the afternoon of an away game. He sat down and I shared a story with him that Dr. Jim Loehr shared with me. I drew two rectangles on a sheet of paper.

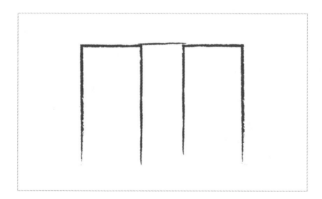

I told him, "Imagine these are two sixty-story skyscrapers. Thirty yards separate the buildings. There's a wooden plank that's twenty-four inches wide that connects the buildings. They asked some high achievers, 'Would you walk across the wooden plank (with nothing supporting you) for one million dollars?' Only 5% of the people that were asked said yes. Why do you think that is?"

Tyler said, "They didn't think it was worth it to risk their life for money."

Me: You got it. They then changed the story. They asked the group, "Would you walk across the plank if it was the only way to save your family's life?" What do you think the group said?

Tyler: Yes.

Me: 100% of the people said that they would. What's the difference?

Tyler: The purpose for doing it.

The task was the same, but the reason for doing it was different. When you are doing something for a reason outside of yourself—you strengthen your purpose.

After we talked about that, I shared a story of mine with Tyler. I told him that when I was a sophomore in high school I was a decent player. I started varsity and averaged about 16 points a game. There was a moment that changed everything for me.

My grandpa passed away the night before the district semifinal game. My mom went to be with her family, but we decided that it would be best if I played the game. That's what Papa (my grandpa) would want. I did. What happened next is hard to explain.

I dedicated that game to my grandpa and I had 46 points that night. Up until that point, I had never had a performance like that. From that point on I dedicated every game of my high school career to my grandpa. I carried a picture of him in my bag and before games I would say a few words to him. When you have a purpose outside of yourself, it allows you to play inspired.

Dear Coach

This is where motivation (the purpose for doing something) and appreciation meet. Blakely's team was playing against a top-10 team in the country on the road. She had a lot of things that were going on in her personal life. We used the skill of appreciation to help motivate her. I handed her this card.

GAME DEDICATION
Today I'm playing for you.

_____

_____

_____

_____

_____

I asked her to dedicate the game to someone that was really important to her. She did. She dedicated it to her coach. Check out what she wrote:

Dear Coach,

I am giving tonight's game to you. Other people would dedicate it to their family, a close friend, or someone important to them, but I wanted to do all three, so I chose you. (You have an extra one, though because you're my coach too :)

I know you are my coach so we see each other every day, but I never thank you for everything you have been doing for me. I never tell you how much you impact me. Yes, you have made me a much better player. But you have also made me an even better person. Your support, love, and unconditional acceptance of everything means the world to me.

Through all of this chaos that I've been going through, you have been so supportive. You've guided me in the right direction to becoming a better person. This may sound kind of weird, but I believe this whole experience has helped me find myself. I think that you truly need to be alone in order to find yourself, and for me, it wasn't necessarily by choice, but I am thankful that I have been put through this adversity because I have become a better me.

I am so thankful to be a part of this team—it truly is something special. The support of twenty-four sisters and four amazing parents (coaches) around me—well…there's no better family than that. I am blessed to have you as my coach, support system, and family. I am giving tonight's game to you. Thank you for everything you have done (and continue to do) for me…day in and day out.

-Blakely

What an amazing letter. Guess what happened during the game? The score is 0–0 after 84 minutes of play. (College soccer games are 90 minutes.) During that 84th minute, Blakely gets a shot on goal and connects. She scores the game-winning goal.

After the game, she runs over to her coach. They embrace. Tears are shed and the coach says, "Thank you for doing that for me."

Isn't that an amazing story? When you play for a purpose that's outside of yourself it's amazing the performance that you can get.

I shared this story with a high-level swimming coach. I told him that I thought it'd be a great exercise to help his team with the upcoming conference tournament. He wanted to find something that would release the pressure that comes with the event.

He asked, "Wouldn't that create more pressure on them?"

Me: I think it converts the tournament from a threat to an opportunity.

Coach: How?

Me: Instead of feeling the pressure of letting people down, we repurpose the meet into an opportunity to honor someone (that is really important in their life) through their performance.

Dear Grandma

After sharing Blakely's story with Tyler I asked him, "Who's the most important person in your life?"

Tyler said, "My grandma."

I asked him to write a dedication letter to her. Here's what he wrote:

Dear Grandma,

I don't think that you know how much you mean to me. You have taught me so many different things throughout my life. Every time something was bad I always knew that if I called you—you would be there. I always knew that no matter what, me and my momma would have a place to stay if we got kicked out of the house and we didn't have anywhere to go.

You have shaped me into the young man that I am today. You taught me how to treat people the right way, you taught me how to pray, and you showed me how to forgive the people who might've hurt me growing up (mom and dad).

You know that I don't ever show any of my emotions, but I just want you to know that I really love you with all of my heart. I am so thankful to have you as my grandmother and you are my role model. One more thing, without you grandma I would not be the person I am today. You motivate me to be the best person and player that I can be. I am going to dedicate this game to you tonight. I love you!

Love,
Tyler

Tyler got really emotional (as did I). Tears hit the page as he read those words to me. I told him, "Those words gave me goose bumps. I can't imagine what those words are going to make your grandma feel."

Tyler: (Crying) I've never told her this before.

I gave Tyler his space and he called his grandma and read her the letter he had written her.

That night Tyler dedicated the game to his grandma. Do you remember back to the Courage section? Tyler drew a green dot on his arm sleeve to help him reset and "play green." That night Tyler wrote his grandma's initials on the inside of his green dot to remind him *who* he was playing for. He took a picture of it before the game and sent her the picture.

Thank You, Setbacks

Expressing gratitude is a great way to show appreciation. I was working with a high-level volleyball team. I had everybody in the room write a thank-you note to a setback in their life.

One player wrote a note to her mother.

Thank you for abandoning me in my younger years. It made me grow and mature quicker than I had to. You made me become more dependent on myself. After all of the years that you neglected me and refused to talk to me, you made me realize that instead of focusing on what I don't have, I need to cherish the strong relationships that I do have.

Another player wrote a note to their "freshman year in college." They traveled across the country to pursue their career as an athlete. They realized some things very quickly:

Thank you for making me realize how much I loved my home. Thank you for showing me that I wish I saw my parents more. It made me so sad to leave knowing that I didn't do that all along. Lastly, thank you for showing me who wanted to stay in my life and who was just there for the time being.

One of the things that I believe to my core is: *everything in life is balanced*. Even in really bad situations, there are great things that come out of them. For example, the player that had an absent mother was forced to become self-reliant at an early age. That has significantly contributed to her confidence levels (self-trust).

When you look at things from this perspective, you realize that every moment you encounter is a moment to make you better. Appreciate the moment and how it contributes to the person that you want to become.

Unexpected Gratitude

Everybody on the volleyball team wrote a thank-you note to a struggle except one person. I had the team captain, who was a walk-on, write a thank-you note to the most influential person in her life. I was a little deceptive in order to make the exercise work. Her name was Erin.

I talked with Erin before the presentation, "I need you to bring your phone into the film room today. We are going to do something cool with our thank-you notes. I need you to demonstrate how to share the pictures with your phone."

Erin, a little confused, replied, "OK."

After the team wrote their thank-you notes, I called Erin up to the front of the room. I said, "Erin can you explain why you are up front?"

She said, "We are going to do something with our notes. I'm going to demonstrate how while Brett talks."

Me: Let's call an audible. I had you write a different thank-you note, right?

Erin: Yes. I wrote a note to the most influential person in my life.

Me: Who'd you write it to?

Erin: My dad.

Me: Here's what's going to happen. We aren't going to take pictures. The reason you have your phone is because you are going to call your dad and read what you wrote to him.

Erin: (Blushing)

What I didn't know was how big of an influence he had on the rest of the team. Everybody loved Erin's dad. Erin called her dad and put him on speaker. She read the following:

Thank you for always being my biggest supporter. You are not only an amazing father, you are an amazing person. I have learned so much from you by how you live your life. You have inspired me in all aspects of life. You taught me that I am strong enough to overcome any obstacle in my life. I know I can accomplish anything because you believe in me. You have always encouraged me to see the big picture. You are a father figure for so many people because they trust you completely. I hope one day that I can be an influential parental figure like you.

It was hard for Erin to get through her letter because she became very emotional. By the end of the letter there wasn't a dry eye in the room. I believe in that moment the players saw the power of appreciation. Unexpected gratitude sneaks up on people. If Erin would have written that to him on a birthday card, it might not have meant as much because he might expect a sentimental gesture.

I joked to Erin, "He probably thought you were calling because you needed money. What a great surprise." Erin smiled… while crying. It was awesome.

Thanks to Tournament Director

I was talking with a parent of a very high-level athlete. I'm amazed by his son's ability to handle all of the attention that comes from being dominant at his sport. He's exceptional. The dad told me that he told his son, "The people that you see on the way up will be the same people that you will see on your way down. Show appreciation to everybody that helps you no matter how insignificant that help may seem, because you will see them again."

That's great advice and it's funny because a few days later I was having a conversation with a high-level tennis coach named Bryan who validates that message.

Bryan: You know what my parents made me do after every tennis tournament?

Me: What?

Bryan: Write a thank-you note to every tournament director of any tournament that I ever played in.

Me: That's awesome.

Bryan: I used to hate it. Then I realized something. When I was a pro and my ranking started to go down—I wasn't qualifying for tournaments. The tournament directors were allowed to elect three wild cards. I had a great reputation with them because I had written all those "thank-yous" and because of that, they would elect me for those positions.

Showing appreciation extended Bryan's career when his age and athleticism started to decline. What can we learn from that? When somebody helps you and takes interest in you, show them appreciation. Chances are you will see them again.

ETM

Have you ever heard somebody say, "Enjoy the journey?" I asked Blakely that question and she responded, "Yes."

I then asked, "Why do you think people struggle with doing that?"

Blakely: I think people struggle with this because they are constantly looking beyond where they are currently living. It's hard to focus on what is right in front of you without worrying or thinking about the future or the "next thing." People always say, "Live in the moment," but how can you fully live and exist in that moment if your mind is somewhere else?

I show a lot of players Blakely's response and they can relate to that. It became very important to me to try and find a way to help Blakely enjoy her journey. I asked her (on a Tuesday), "What's the best thing that happened to you last Wednesday?"

Blakely said (laughing), "I don't remember what happened last week."

Me: How can we enjoy the journey if we don't remember the moments?

Blakely: Good point.

Me: You know what I love?

Blakely: What?

Me: Peanut M&M's. When I get a bag of M&M's I devour it until I get down to the last three. Then, you know what I do? I eat them one by one. I suck on them until the chocolate melts and all I'm left with is the peanut. It takes me longer to eat the last three than it does to eat the rest of the bag. Can you relate to that?

Blakely: (Laughing) I do that too.

Here's what I did. I gave her a jar of 63 peanut M&M's the next day. Why 63? There were 63 days until the national championship game was going to be played. She was going to eat one a day. Here was the goal: as she savors the M&M she was going to write down in a journal the best moment that she shared with her team that day.

At the end of each week she could then reflect on the past week and see all of the great moments that she shared with her team. Do you see how that would help her enjoy the journey more as she reflects and appreciates all of the great moments that she shared with the people she cares about?

On the cover of her journal it reads ETM. Enjoy The Moment.

5 Ways to Exercise Appreciation

1. **Recognize Your Teammates:**
   You can't do anything without the help of your teammates, coaches, and the program that helped put you in a position to do what you do. Take time to appreciate all of those people. Whether it's like the example from above: pointing to your teammate after making a shot, or something else, find ways inside your sport to

increase your appreciation levels.

2. **Dedication Letters:**
   Use your sport to honor the people in your life that are important to you. Blakely honored her coach for being her support system during her difficult times. Tyler used his sport to honor his grandma. You can write them a letter explaining how they've impacted your life. Then, you can find ways to bring them into the game. Tyler did that by writing his grandma's initials inside the green dot. He took a picture and sent it to her.

3. **Thank-You, Setback:**
   Expressing gratitude is a great way to exercise appreciation. When you show thankfulness towards someone or something—you force yourself to appreciate the good side of the equation. Even if the situation is tough (e.g. growing up without your mom) by writing a thank-you note it helps you pull out the good from the situation.

4. **Unexpected Gratitude:**
   Erin surprised her dad by calling him and reading him a note that she had written to him. It had a profound impact on Taylor, her dad, and the team as they listened to her read it to him. Think about your inner circle or your board of directors—start your day by surprising someone with unexpected gratitude.

5. **ETM Journal:**
   Start a journal. End each day by writing down the best thing that happened to you that day. At the end of each week, take some time to reflect. Review all of the great

moments that you experienced with the people that you care about.

If you are planning on using M&M's as an incentive to remind you—I would store them in a place where chocolate doesn't melt!

☑ Caring

Warning: contains explicit language.

I asked Kenny, "When you're around your teammates do you talk about surface level stuff?"

He responded, "Yeah."

Me: Why don't you talk about your struggles?

Kenny: The guys I grew up with don't really talk about stuff like that.

Me: Why not?

Kenny: You don't want to look soft. You just learn to cover your emotions up.

Win For Them

I was talking with a player, "Do you agree that if you had a team full of players that cared about each other, it would make the team better?

The player responded, "No doubt."

When you can get a team to play for each other it's amazing to see how they take off.

Anson Dorrance, women's soccer coach at the University of North Carolina, has figured out a way to do that. His teams have played in (and won) over 20 National Championships. The night before his team plays, he writes a handwritten letter to every senior on the team.

He waits to write these letters the night before the game because he wants to be immersed in the emotional space that comes along with playing in a national championship game.

Here's his itinerary:

11:00 p.m.: He starts writing his notes to all of the seniors.

3:00–5:00 a.m.: Finishes the letters. His manager photocopies all of the notes and slides them under each door to the rooms of the seniors.

8:00 a.m.: Seniors wake up to handwritten notes from their head coach.

Anson keeps photocopies of all the notes that he's writ-ten and he reads each note in the locker room during the pregame speech. Each note captures the essence of their character—who they've become *as a person* during their time at the University of North Carolina.

Anson told me, "There's not a dry eye in the locker room" at the conclusion of reading these notes.

Imagine being in that locker room as a player. How amazing would that experience be?

After the underclassmen hear these notes, they understand their mission. Their mission: win for the seniors.

You know what's interesting? Anson has a higher winning percentage playing in national championship games than any other part of the season. (His career winning percentage is above 90%.) Think about it. It all comes down to purpose. The underclassmen want to win for their seniors.

A powerful combination happens when striving for excellence meets doing it with (and for) those you care about.

Relationship versus Mastery

I'm working with four really high-level basketball players who are in high school. All four will play college basketball at the highest level. Something really interesting happened the last time we met. After our training session concluded, all four of them stuck around afterwards.

This is what was happening at one end of the gym:

Napheesa (to the left) and Cierra (to the right) were using a basketball to play volleyball. Ci would use a basketball to bounce the other ball back to Napheesa. Together they would see how many volleys they could get in a row. Notice the collaboration—they are working together.

Something much different was happening on the other end. They were playing one-on-one.

I looked back down to the girl's side and guess what they were doing? (I'm not creative enough to make this up.)

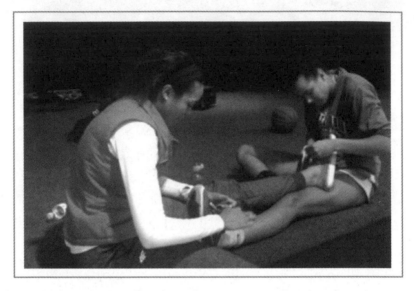

They were tying each other shoes. Again, they're showing collaboration. (They had no idea I was filming.)

Relationship-Driven

I had a conversation with Napheesa, the player on the left, about this:

Me: Why don't you and Ci ever play 1v1?

Napheesa: If she had asked me to—I would. But it's not fun for me.

Me: I thought you loved to compete at basketball?

Napheesa: I love competing with other people. When you're on a team—you are working with your teammates to win. That's the part that I enjoy.

Me: Why do you think guys are more likely to play 1v1 and girls aren't?

Napheesa: Guys are constantly trying to prove who's better. They'll say, 'I beat you at 1v1' to prove themselves. If a girl said that, people would be like, 'Nobody cares.'

Mastery-Driven

I was having a conversation with an alpha-male. I asked him to consider this question: In a televised event who would you rather beat?

Option 1: Your rival at 1v1
Option 2: Beat your rival's team

He started laughing and then he asked me, "Do you want the honest answer?"

Me: Yes.

Player: Option 1.

Me: (Laughing)

Player: I want everybody to know who's better individually.

The only thing that matters to this player is: When people who watch the game leave, do they think that I'm better than my rival? A team win would cloud that judgment. In a 1v1 game there is no mistake about who proved dominance.

Think back to the Competitive section. Do you remember the dysfunctional culture? How did they define being competitive? They originally looked at it as:

Strive to win something by defeating or establishing superiority over others who are trying to do the same thing.

If you are trying *to defeat and establish superiority* over each other, how can a good relationship (based on care) flourish in an environment where people don't want to see each other do well?

Do you see how that could get in the way of a relationship? Here's what I've noticed (regardless of gender): players that are mastery-driven struggle with interacting with people that are relationship-driven. On the flip side, players that are relationship-driven struggle with interacting with people that are mastery-driven.

Social Norms

I've had the privilege of working with both men and women. Through my experience I've noticed that it's more common for females to be driven by relationships and males to be driven by mastery. But I have also worked with mastery-driven females and relationship-driven males.

I was talking with Dr. Harry Edwards about what was happening on the guy's side of the court (from the example above).

Harry taught the sociology of sport at the University of California, Berkeley for 33 years. He had 400 spots in his classroom and every semester there were 1,600 people that signed up for his course. It was the highest attended course in sociology.

I shared with him the photos from above. (He chuckled.) I asked him, "Why does this happen?"

Harry: A lot of men feel like the route to survival is by dominating the other guy. That's how they were conditioned. They're establishing dominance—my game is better than yours.

Me: Do a lot of the men that you work with struggle with what care looks like?

Harry: Absolutely. A lot of them come from environments where people don't care about them as a person. Coaches, teachers, parents, media, cops, and agent runners care about what they can bring to the table. Care is a foreign concept for a lot of them.

Here's the definition that we work from when we use the word caring.

Caring: Investing in the person.
(Not just the player.)

What You're Up Against

I was brought in to work with a dysfunctional team. During one of the presentations, I handed each player a survey (featured later in this section) and I put them into groups of three. I had them ask each other questions from the survey. As they started to interview each other I listened in. One player asked another, "What's your most prized possession?" The player responded, "My dick."

Another player asked his teammate, "What's your favorite hobby outside of sport?" The teammate responded, "Having sex." Everybody in the room laughed (including the coaches). I was totally conflicted because I value my time and clearly this team wasn't taking the exercise seriously.

Instead of meeting that comment with judgment, I wanted to understand why that happened. Obviously he didn't see the value in getting to know his teammates on a deeper level. The next day I brought in one of his teammates and I asked, "Why do you think the culture is set up in a way where it's difficult for caring relationships to exist?"

He responded, "Last year I was talking with coach at a team meal. I told him about my high school team. I said it was more like a brotherhood."

The coach then said, "So basically you're telling me that you played with a bunch of pussies." He said that in front of the whole team. Everybody laughed *except the person who brought it up.* He was humiliated.

Is it any wonder why this player's teammate would answer that way about his most prized possession? He's developed a defense mechanism to help him not show any weakness. Why wouldn't he do that? If he were to express his feelings he would risk being humiliated in front of his peers.

When I share that story with women they're like *"Yep. I've dated a few guys like that."*

I was talking with a high-level men's team about this.

I asked, "Do you agree that if talent is the same, the team that is most connected will win? Like, do you think that matters?"

The team nodded their head yes.

I then asked, "If I were to walk into your locker room and listen to the conversations—would I hear a bunch of surface-level conversations about how many people you hook-up with?"

You could tell that's exactly what they talked about.

I then asked, "If you never talk about anything of substance or express care—how could strong connections exist?"

One player spoke for the team, "They can't."

I then asked, "Then why don't you express how you feel towards each other?"

Another player said, "You don't want people to think you're soft."

There's strength in expressing care. Unfortunately, in some cultures it's very difficult for that to happen.

Conditional Care

I was having a conversation with a mastery-driven female. She was having a tough time connecting with her teammates. She told me that she only invests in the players that can help her win. Consider this conversation that we had:

Bri: I really struggle communicating with my teammates.

Me: Why?

Bri: I just want my teammates to show up and do their job because that's what I do. I hate to admit this, but I care more about the players who can help me win.

Me: Why?

Bri: I probably do that because that's how my dad treated me. Our relationship was good when I played good and bad when I played bad.

Is it any wonder why Bri struggles with having good relationships? Bri cares about performance. Her care is conditional. She doesn't care about who her teammates are *as people.* She cares about who can help her win. Bri was socialized this way. Her dad was nice to her when she played good and was the opposite when she played bad. His affection was based on her performance.

All of the signals that Bri's been sent are signals that would lead her to believe that her value comes from her athletic achievement.

Me: Do you really want to build meaningful relationships with people that you care about?

Bri: Yes. But I don't even know where to start.

Together we started to explore what that looks like. I gave her five tools.

Tool: The Personal Survey

Great relationships aren't conditional. In other words, if you really care about someone—it's not contingent upon his or her performance. The only way to have caring relationships is to separate the person from the player. Here's a great lesson from a coach that players can learn from.

Charlie Strong is a high-level football coach at the University of Texas. He strives to get to know each individual *as a person* versus just as a player. Every freshman that comes into his program gets a survey. Here are the 25 questions:

1. Name(s) of parent(s) or guardian(s)?
2. Names & age(s) of brother(s) and/or sister(s)?
3. Who else in your family is very involved with you?
4. Who has been the most influential person in your life and why?
5. Who are you most proud of and why?
6. Describe the happiest event in your life.
7. Describe the saddest day in your life.
8. What are your goals in life?
9. What is the most embarrassing thing that has happened to you?
10. What was your greatest personal athletic moment?
11. If you could have dinner with any three people living or dead, who would they be?
12. When was the last time you cried and why?
13. What was the major reason you came to this university?
14. What awards have you won?
15. If you could bring anything from your hometown (to our campus) what would it be?
16. What is your most prized possession?
17. What is your favorite activity?
18. What is your least favorite activity?
19. Do you have any nicknames?
20. What is the name of the best book you have ever read?
21. What is your hobby outside of sport?
22. Do you have any superstitions?
23. What word in the dictionary would your picture appear next to?

24. If you could trade places with someone for a day, who would it be and why?
25. What did you dream of being when you were young?

There are football coaches at the highest level who don't know all of their player's names because they carry such big rosters. Think about that for a second. Can you imagine being in a culture where a coach calls you by a number instead of by your name?

That sounds like, "Number 54 come over here. I need to talk to you." Why wouldn't the player feel like just a number in this situation?

As a player if you want to have good sustainable relationships with your teammates, the first thing that you have to do is separate the person from the player and get to know them as a person.

This survey is a great tool—am I saying that you should sit down with a teammate and ask them all of these questions? No. They might think you're weird if your coach isn't driving it. But you could pull a few questions out and casually bring them up in conversation.

Tool: Meet the Buckeyes

I asked Thad Matta, who coaches basketball at The Ohio State University, "What's the best team-building activity that you guys do?" He told me about an activity that they call "Meet the Buckeyes." He explains:

You partner up your players with each other. They have to know everything about the other guy and have to tell the circle about this guy…from family, to faith, to what motivates him, to their fears—just who they are as a person. It becomes very emotional for kids to talk about it.

But at that point, I think it lets everybody know that each guy in this room is trying to get somewhere but each guy in this room has issues along the way and that we know what's important.

Do you see how this could help your team chemistry? If the answer is yes, could you talk to your coach to see if they would be open to doing this? You could use some of the questions from the personal survey (above example) as a starting point to get to know your teammate.

You know what's cool about the "Meet The Buckeyes" exercise? You actually present what you find to the team about the teammate you were partnered with. It's a great way to get everybody on the same page.

Tool: Circle-Ups

Before Ohio State takes the court for practice, Thad Matta has what he calls Circle-Ups. The players on the team stand or sit in a circle. The idea: the guys in this circle are the only people that affect the result we're chasing.

The circle prevents outside forces from penetrating the team. If players are struggling with something, it's brought up. For example, if a player's grandmother passes away—they deal with it…together. If a player's parent is pressuring him by asking, "Why aren't you playing more?" It's brought up.

Anything that could get in the way of the team is brought up so they can confront issues together. Think about how much more connected a team would be because of that. As a result, think about how much better practice would be.

When your teammates want to win for the person next to them more than they want to win for themselves—that is a powerful force. What if you talked to your coach about organizing circle-ups with the team? Do you see how that would help you build connection?

Tool: The Care Chart

I was working with a player that wanted to invest more in his teammates *as people* versus just as athletes. I shared this idea with him. He loved the idea. We created a chart like this:

WEEKLY CARE CHART							
TEAMMATES	SUNDAY	MONDAY	TUESDAY	WEDNESDAY	THURSDAY	FRIDAY	SATURDAY

You could use this chart. On the left side you could fill your teammates' names in. Then across the top of the chart are the days of the week. Sunday–Saturday. Your goal: invest in every one of your teammates at least once a week. Each time you invest in your teammates as people, put a check mark in their box.

You can track who you're investing in and who you aren't.

List out the opportunities that you have to invest in your teammates. A few examples:

- Sitting with them on the bus ride to an away game.
- Taking them out to your team meal.
- Sitting with them in the bleachers before a home game.

When you are with them—focus on them. Find ways that you can learn about and support them away from sport.

Caring = Investing in the person. (Not just the player.)

How can you invest in the person?

Tool: Tracking Touches

I believe that every time we touch, energy is exchanged. There was a wonderful study done by Dacher Keltner and a team of researchers that found the teams that touch the most, win the most. The research was conducted with NBA teams. Dacher told me touch increases trust and lowers stress levels. It's how they measured the connection of a team.

Before every training session in our academy, I pull over a player (in private) and I tell them they have one job for the day. Their job: 25 touches with their teammates. High-fives. Shoulder bumps. Arm around the shoulder.

You know what we've found? It's contagious. When I tell a player, "Alright you have 25 touches." Once they start handing them out, what starts to happen? Everybody starts to do it.

Touch is linked to the connection that you have with your teammates. A great leader once told me, "The best leaders are able to kick someone in the ass with their arm around their shoulder."

As a player, how could you strategically inject the power of touch to express care within the context of your sport?

5 Ways to Exercise Care

1. **Reposition Your View:**
   Care is the foundation of successful, meaningful relationships. Use the team concept to begin to understand what goes into a caring relationship. Change the way you view care. Instead of viewing the expression of emotions as a weakness—view it as a strength that will form a strong connection between you and your teammates.

2. **Get to Know the Person:**
   Charlie Strong gives each player a survey when they come in—all the questions are centered around who they are as a person. Thad Matta said his best team-building exercise is "Meet The Buckeyes." Could you talk to your coach and try to do either of those activities with your team?

   Care is unconditional. It's not contingent on what someone brings to the table. That's why it's very important to separate the person from the player with your teammates. Caring is investing in the person (not just the player). The only way you can do that is to get to know your teammates as people.

3. **Opportunities For Care:**
   Look for opportunities to show people that you care.

List out the different ways that you could display that to each of your teammates. By getting to know your teammates away from your sport—you'll have a better idea of who they are. Once you understand their story you can find different ways that you can invest in them.

4. **Care Chart:**
   Track your progress. Make a care chart to help you understand the investments that you are making in your teammates.

   Each day you invest in your teammate check their box. Make a goal (depending on the roster size): invest once a week in each teammate. Whether it's sitting next to them on the bus or having a conversation post practice. Find different ways to invest in your teammates. Build those things into your daily habits.

5. **Touches:**
   What does touch do? It increases trust and decreases stress. Make it your goal to give out 25 touches (high fives, shoulder bumps, etc.) to your teammates each practice. Watch how contagious it is—it's awesome.

After Kenny and I finished laying the foundation of character skills that he was going to be working on, we had a conversation. I asked him, "What do you take away from our time together?"

He responded, "Separate who you are from what you do. Your character drives everything. I know that if I focus on growing as a person that I'll improve as a player and I'll get better results."

Me: Favorite lesson?

Kenny: I don't think I can pick just one. It's crazy because you think you know what something means and then you learn more about it and it's like *I never thought about it like that before.*

Me: How are you going to keep it going?

Kenny: I like the accountability card idea. That will help me focus on what I need to do on a daily basis to make sure that I become the person to my teammates and coaches that I want to be. I need to have somebody on my board of directors that's in charge of my accountability cards.

I smiled when he told me that. Kenny and I got to know one another on a deeper level. I identified with him. We shared the same story. I will always cherish the time I spent learning with him. A few weeks after our meetings concluded—he sent me this letter.

Dear Brett,

Do you remember the first thing you said to me? You asked me, "Why are we meeting?" You threw me for a loop—I was doing it because my coach said to trust you. After meeting with you a few times I realized that it was really going to help me.

Where I grew up, everybody viewed me as an athlete first. I never really even thought about who I was without my sport. You helped me understand the relationship that I had with my sport better. I realized that my self-worth was tied to my results. I thought that's how I provided value to people. I now know that basketball is what I do, it's not who I am.

A few meetings in you asked me, "Why do you trust me?" I had a tough time putting into words how I felt. I know now. I never felt judged by you—it was like you just wanted to understand my perspective.

You do ask a lot of questions though. At first I didn't know how to take it. But I learned that the reason you asked me those questions was to get me to understand myself better.

I know you're busy and I really appreciate you taking time to help me find out about who I am as a person. You don't know how much this helped me. Thank you.

-Kenny

Closing Acknowledgements:

This project is the result of many conversations. I would like to thank all of these wonderful people who have helped me understand what drives winning on a deeper level.

Mike Anderson	Neil Dougherty
Geno Auriemma	Kevin Durant
Emily Bastel	Carol Dweck
John Beilein	Harry Edwards
Tony Bennett	Sue Enquist
Marvin Berkowitz	David Epstein
Jay Bilas	Rhonda Faehn
Chauncey Billups	Mark Few
Jim Boeheim	Brenda Frese
Brenda Bredemeier	Michael Gervais
Mike Brey	Blake Griffin
Becky Burleigh	John Handrigan
Tamika Catchings	James Harden
Tyson Chandler	Bria Hartley
Jack Clark	Gordan Hayward
Sherri Coale	Mike Holloway
Mike Conley	Andre Iguodala
Daniel Coyle	Kyrie Irving
Steph Curry	Tom Izzo
Mark Daigneault	DeAndre Jordan
Anthony Davis	Dacher Keltner
JC Deacon	Mike Krzyzewski
Billy Donovan	Damian Lillard
Anson Dorrance	Jim Loehr

(continued on next page)

Kevin Love

Thad Matta

Joanne McCallie

Angel McCougherty

Muffet McGraw

Teri Mckeever

Bob McKillop

Don Meyer

Maya Moore

Matt Painter

Candace Parker

Chandler Parsons

Carolyn Peck

Clark Powers

Lorenzo Romar

Derrick Rose

Bill Self

Bryan Shelton

David Shields

Shaka Smart

Marcus Smart

Brad Stevens

Charlie Strong

Tom Thibodeau

Klay Thompson

Roland Thornqvist

Gregg Troy

Dick Vitale

John Wall

Tim Walton

Abby Wambach

Russell Westbrook

Lyndsey Whalen

Monty Williams

Deron Williams

Roy Williams

Buzz Williams

Mary Wise

Steve Wojciechowski

Jay Wright

Interested in learning more?
Visit WhatDrivesWinning.com
– and –
FilmroomProject.org